D0114059

earth
Angels

stories of
heavenly encouragement
through *earthly* vessels

susan duke

HOWARD
PUBLISHING CO.

*O*ur purpose at Howard Publishing is to:

- *Increase faith* in the hearts of growing Christians
- *Inspire holiness* in the lives of believers
- *Instill hope* in the hearts of struggling people everywhere

 Because He's coming again!

Earth Angels © 2002 by Susan Duke
All rights reserved. Printed in the United States of America

Published by Howard Publishing Co., Inc.
3117 North 7th Street, West Monroe, Louisiana 71291-2227

02 03 04 05 06 07 08 09 10 11   10 9 8 7 6 5 4 3 2 1

Edited by Michele Buckingham
Interior design by Stephanie Denney

Library of Congress Cataloging-in-Publication Data
Duke, Susan.
    Earth angels : stories of heavenly encouragement through earthly vessels /
Susan Duke.
        p. cm.
    Includes bibliographical references (p.).
    ISBN: 1-58229-216-7
      1. Christian life. I. Title.

BV4515.3 .D85 2002
242—dc21

                                                                  2001039997

Scripture quotations not otherwise marked are taken from the Holy Bible, New International Version. Copyright © 1973, 1978, 1984 International Bible Society. Used by permission of Zondervan Bible Publishers. Other Scriptures are quoted from The Holy Bible, Authorized King James Version (KJV), © 1961 by The National Publishing Co.

DEDICATION

I lovingly dedicate this book to
the earth angels in my life.
You have graced my heart with more love
than I could ever be worthy of.

To Harvey, my husband and soul mate. Thank you
for loving me unconditionally, believing in me, and giving me the freedom to follow my dreams. I'm certain my
real guardian angel applauds you for all the times you've
picked up my drooping, earthly wings and straightened
my slightly crooked halo. Your faith in my writing keeps
me soaring with enthusiasm and gives me the courage to

write from my heart. You are the wind beneath my wings.

To Kelly, my beloved daughter and friend. Your strength, encouragement, and love mean everything to me. You continually fill my heart with sunshine and flowers. I could not have been blessed with a more precious daughter. You will always be my baby girl.

To Thomas, my beloved son and borrowed angel for eighteen years. You are the shining star of my heart. Even now from your heavenly home, you are teaching me that love is the invisible bridge between heaven and earth. I can hardly wait to see you again.

To Mama, who gave me life and the invaluable gifts of laughter and determination. Your example of optimism and joy has inspired me to become an earth angel of encouragement to others. No one can take your place in my heart.

To Kara, Noah, Tyler, Rachel, Angela, Anthony, Todd, Tara, Aaron, Ryan, Dorinda, Dana, Brenda, and Linda. Thank you for every hug, every giggle, and every precious affirmation of love you have deposited deep within my heart. You are my treasures.

To my sisters and brothers, nieces, nephews, and in-laws. The bond and memories we share are forever. Your

dedication

love and the bountiful blessings of family have helped my heart find its voice.

To my earth-angel friends. You know who you are. Without you, many of the stories in this book would not have been written. You are my inspiration—the earthly vessels who've enriched and changed my life. If I fly on a wing and a prayer, it's because you've lent me your wings and whispered the prayers. God knew my life would not be complete without you.

Most of all, *to my Lord and Savior, Jesus Christ,* from whom all blessings flow. You are my source for everything —my dream maker and my vision keeper. You are the one who put heaven's pen in my hand. In You alone do I live and move and have my being. Thank You for loving me just as I am and allowing me every now then— tattered wings and all—to be an earth angel to some of Your kids. I give You all the glory.

CONTENTS

a SURPRISE tribute
TO AN EARTH angel

They are all around us, scattered here and there, seemingly always at the right place at the right time as if by divine appointment. They often come disguised as store clerks, postal workers, factory employees, teachers, nurses, truck drivers, housewives, or even children. On certain occasions you may have entertained one of them, completely unaware of their deeds of compassion and kindness. They would never boast about their acts of love. They just quietly go about doing good whenever the opportunity presents itself.

They are angels—earth angels. They are earthly vessels

overflowing with heavenly encouragement. They are ordinary people distributing love and compassion to their neighbors. They are helpers, givers, and supporters.

In my lifetime I have been privileged to meet a few of these earth angels. But there is one in particular I have come to know best. She is my friend. Humility is her trademark. She never seeks recognition or reward for her frequent acts of kindness. She doesn't brag about how she has helped or encouraged someone in need. She never wants any glory for being the servant she is. She possesses a God-given heart of love for the hurting. And from that heart springs compassion—for compassion is the constant companion of love.

During the years I have known her, I have often seen her wash many a troubled soul in a warm shower of God's healing love. I have watched her impart a sense of renewed hope, faith, and love as only one of God's true earth angels can.

If you have guessed who this special earth angel is and who has penned these words of praise, you might think I've written from a biased point of view. Perhaps—just a little. But if you knew this earth angel as I do, you would know I haven't missed the mark.

Who is she? She is my helpmate, my companion. She is also the author of this book. She is my own very special earth angel. She is my wife.

To Susan, with my heartfelt expression of love.

Your husband,

Harvey

P.S. Susan never knew until *Earth Angels* was published that these words would be included in her book. Thanks to Philis Boultinghouse, Susan's editor at Howard Publishing, for allowing me to express them.

ACKNOWLEDGMENTS

To John Howard, Denny Boultinghouse, Gary Myers, and all of the wonderful staff at Howard Publishing whose trust, dedication, and expertise made this project possible.

A special heartfelt thanks to Philis Boultinghouse, my esteemed and gracious editor, who enthusiastically affirmed the vision for *Earth Angels* and made me believe it could really fly.

To all who encouraged me to write my stories, I can't thank you enough for attaching wings to my dreams. And to all who so willingly opened your hearts and gave me permission to write your stories, words cannot express how you've touched my life.

But we have

this treasure

in earthen vessels,

that the excellency

of the power

may be of God,

and not of us.

—2 Corinthians 4:7 KJV

I shall not pass this way again;
Then let me now relieve some pain,
Remove some barrier from the road,
Or brighten someone's heavy load.
—Eva Rose York

Introduction

EARNING MY wings

When I was a kid, Mama used to tell me I was an angel with a dirty face. And when someone I'd never met asked her, "Is this your little angel?" she would playfully reply, "Yes, when she's asleep and not dreaming bad dreams."

I wonder if that's why, when I was four years old, she gave me a nickel every day to take a nap! All I knew was that a nickel would buy candy and bubble gum at the corner grocery store. And before naptime was over and Mama missed me, I could be out the window, down the block, and back in bed.

I got away with it—for a while.

Then one fateful day Mama made a trip of her own to Mr. Mosley's store. "Why, Miss Cora, how are you today?" he asked Mama. "I see that cute little Suzie 'most every day at about two-thirty, when she comes in to buy candy!"

The next day on my way back home from the store, whom did I see in the distance, waiting for me in front of the house? Mama. And what was in her hand? A long, freshly picked peach-tree switch.

Needless to say, my days of sneaking out the window to buy candy were over. It didn't matter that I told Mama I was saving some of my candy for friends or that I just couldn't sleep in the afternoons. Although the chances of running into danger in those days were minimal compared to the crime rates today, Mama knew it was still dangerous for a four-year-old to cross a busy street by herself.

Even then, I think angels must have been watching over me. For my own protection, they probably arranged for me to get caught—knowing that my four-year-old cherubic face and blonde curls were no guarantee that I would stay out of mischief. And even though I'm now a grown, forty-something woman, I must confess there's still a lot of that four-year-old candy-store thrill seeker in me. Any guardian angel of mine must wear tennis shoes, because I surely keep whoever is watching over me on his toes!

It has been said that we are not human beings having a spiritual experience, but rather, spiritual beings having a human experience. There's a lot of truth in that statement! Could it be that in our quest for extraordinary spiritual experiences, we often overlook the divine in the ordinary—the touches of heaven right here on earth?

In truth, God's most priceless heavenly gifts are often delivered through the most common of earthly vessels— through ordinary hands and feet, hearts and voices. Most of us have never encountered a celestial angel face to face. Yet we all have crossed paths at one time or another with an earth angel who forever changed or sweetened our lives.

Long ago I gave up any vain childhood ambitions of becoming famous. Any dreams I might have dreamed, driven by the false belief that only the famous have the power in this life to make a difference, have long since been replaced by one solid and sacred truth: God has empowered each of us with a special, life-changing gift.

It's called *encouragement.*

As a child I learned the value of encouragement from my mother. I'll never forget our Saturday downtown shopping trips, when Mama would hold my hand and remind me to smile at the people we encountered along the sidewalk, regardless of their station in life. She made this time like a game and challenged me to see who would return my smile. She also explained, "A simple smile is like sunshine on a rainy day—sunshine someone might need today."

A few decades later, those words still motivate my heart. I believe in angels—the heavenly messengers God puts in charge over us. But I also believe we have a calling to be *earth angels* to one another.

As I've tried to live out the values my mother taught me, I can't say that I've earned any angel wings. But I *have* beamed with joy at the smiles, the laughter, and the sweet tears I've seen when offering a gesture of encouragement to someone in need. The feeling is heavenly! And that to me is the *true* reward.

So if I can lay any claim to fame, gifting, or passion in this life, I want to humbly claim the gift of encouragement, for it is God's power and not my own that is released when I seek to encourage others. Amazing, isn't it? To think that God's awesome, supernatural power can be housed and released through earthly vessels like you and me! And that through that release, others might be set free and encouraged—or at the very least, catch a glimpse of His love!

But then, I shouldn't be surprised. After all, more than a few times God has poured His immeasurable love and tender mercy into my own heart through the encouragement of an earth angel.

These earthly angels have entered my life in the most unlikely places at the most extraordinary moments. And although a real halo may not rest upon their heads, they are angels just the same—earth angels. Like real angels on assignment, they've brought me encouragement and hope when I've needed it the most.

Ever since Mama first taught me about smiles, I've realized that throughout life's journey *encouragement* is a key that unlocks doors—doors of hopelessness, fear, rejection, grief, illness, and unfulfilled dreams. Encouragement allows our hearts to soar on wings of hope, beyond the doors of despair and into a realm of bright promise.

The stories in the pages of this book are not about famous people. They are not about great, winged beings in celestial array. They are true stories about ordinary people like you and me. Some are personal accounts of earth angels who have graced my life or of moments when I've been given the privilege of being an earth angel to someone else. Others are from people who told me their stories—stories that left angel footprints upon my heart and inspired me so much that I had to share them.

Earth Angels is my offering of encouragement to you. If one story evokes remembrances of those earth angels who've helped you through life's struggles—or inspires you to blow the dust off your own halo and become an earth angel to someone in need—then God has fulfilled my dream for this book. May the stories on the pages that follow become angel food for your soul!

Give to him

that asketh thee,

and from him

that would borrow

of thee

turn not

thou away.

—Matthew 5:42 KJV

Let no one ever come to you

without leaving better and happier.

Be the living expression

of God's kindness.

—Mother Teresa

Chapter 1

THE LAST straw

Every morning at 5:00 A.M., Beth brewed the first pot of coffee and waited for the local bakery delivery of fresh donuts and sweet rolls. The small highway motel where she worked as a desk clerk catered mostly to weary, late-night travelers; but nonetheless, Beth enjoyed creating an attractive early morning buffet for the guests.

This morning—the coldest ever recorded in this small town on the Texas panhandle—she carefully adorned the long, metal folding table with a starched white cotton tablecloth, a vase of freshly cut flowers, colorful napkins, a dozen blue pottery mugs, and a tall crystal cake plate that soon would be piled high with bakery sweets.

Just part of the job and true Texas hospitality, Beth surmised with a smile.

The donuts arrived, and Beth continued to arrange the table. She was interrupted, however, by the sound of the jingling bell that hung from the motel's glass entry door. *It's a little early for guests to be coming to the lobby*, she thought.

She turned around to see a burly, unshaven young man in a red plaid jacket standing before her. He was shivering. The cold air had blown in with him, and thirty-mile-an-hour winds shrieked threateningly just outside the heavy glass door. The young stranger attempted to comb his sandy brown, windblown hair with his fingers and then plopped an army green duffel bag on the floor.

"Mornin', ma'am," the young man said softly.

"Mornin'," Beth replied, taking her place behind the front desk and trying to sound coolly professional. Her manager had warned her against befriending highway transients or hitchhikers who might wander into the motel lobby, especially during her midnight to 8:00 A.M. shift. "Can I help you?"

"I've been walking all night. Could I bother you for a cup of hot coffee?"

Beth couldn't fathom anyone walking all night in such bitterly cold temperatures, but the drifter certainly looked as if he'd had a rough night.

"Well, we're not supposed to...well, I've been told...why, yes, of course, go ahead and have some coffee."

Beth was surprised to hear the words come out of her mouth. But despite her determination to follow her manager's orders, a still, small voice inside her seemed to say, *If you don't help him, this could be the last straw.*

Beth thought it strange that she should hear such a thing. What did the "last straw" mean? Was it a supernatural warning to be nice to this man lest he become angry and take out his anger on her and the motel? Did it mean that the man was so weary he might not make it without some refreshment? Beth didn't know, but she was certain of one thing: She was to befriend this man—in spite of the warning and rules she'd always followed to the letter.

Beth stepped boldly from behind the desk and poured the man's coffee into the blue mug he'd picked up. "Please, have a seat," she offered, pointing to a chair near the window. While he sat down, she placed two donuts on a paper plate and put it down on a small table next to him. She watched as the steam from the hot coffee warmed his ruddy face and red, chapped hands.

"Thank you," the highway stranger said, looking up at Beth with tired but grateful eyes.

Beth busied herself with the usual morning duties. She filled up the stir-stick jar and placed it next to the coffeepot, along with the creamer and sugar. She answered the phone, placed an order for paper goods and cold drinks, and rang a few rooms for wake-up calls. Even though she was wary of the man sitting in the chair just a few feet from her, she tried to act calmly and confidently. *God, please give me wisdom and help me to do the right thing*, she prayed under her breath. *No one is here but me, so please protect me and keep me safe. Amen.*

"These are surely good donuts," the young man commented.

"I'm glad you like them," Beth answered, deliberately keeping her reply short.

"Thank you for your kindness, ma'am. My name is Samuel. I didn't catch yours."

"Beth. My name is Beth—and you're welcome."

"Is there a restroom close-by where I might wash my hands and face?"

Beth knew she should say no. But either fear or faith made her answer, "Sure, right around the corner. I just put out fresh towels."

"Thank you, Beth. I'll just wash up and be on my way," Samuel said, seeming to sense her uneasiness. Was she detecting a hint of reassurance in his tone? As rough as Samuel appeared, there was something about his demeanor that filled Beth with compassion.

While Samuel occupied the restroom, Beth found two small paper sacks and a large Styrofoam cup beneath the counter. She wrapped up four donuts and two cinnamon rolls and placed them in one of the sacks. Then she filled the tall cup with hot coffee, placed a lid on top, and put it (along with a packet of sugar and creamer) in the other sack. *Am I out of my mind?* Beth asked herself while intently assembling the "to go" care package as sweetly as a mother might prepare her child's lunch. Then she remembered the stickers she'd received in the mail along with an inspirational magazine subscription. Grabbing an envelope from her purse, she retrieved the round, colorful labels imprinted with the words "You are loved (John 3:16)." She folded down the tops of the sacks and secured them with the labels.

When Samuel walked back into the lobby, he picked up his duffel bag and turned to tell Beth "thank you" once again.

"Here," Beth said, reaching across the front desk. "Something for your journey."

For what seemed like a long time, Samuel stared into Beth's eyes. Then he offered a quick smile as he reached for the sacks and tucked them carefully into a side pocket of his duffel bag. Beth watched him walk out the door, through the parking lot, and to the edge of the highway. She was still watching when he turned and waved.

A strange sense of fulfillment warmed Beth's heart that cold November morning. *God,* she prayed again, *I don't know what that was all about. And I admit that it wasn't out of the goodness of my heart that I befriended Samuel. I don't know if I'll ever understand what I heard about "the last straw," but whatever it was, I think I did the right thing. So thank You for giving me the courage to listen and respond. And God…please bless and keep Samuel safe on his journey.*

Since that day, Beth has befriended at least one or two unexpected highway visitors a month. When they ask for a cup of coffee, she serves it joyfully. If they ask for a donut, she gives them two. That still, small voice she so vividly remembers continually inspires her to be a Good Samaritan. Her purse is never without an assortment of cheery stickers, seasonal holiday cards, and loose change for the "honor jar" she contributes to whenever she pours a cup of coffee for a stranger. Beth delights in the surprised expressions of the men and women who walk away from the hotel lobby with goody sacks tucked under their arms.

I met Beth when my husband and I stayed overnight at the Yellow Rose Motel while driving to Colorado last summer. I commented on the long stretch of dark and desolate highway we'd traveled before finally finding a place to spend the night.

"Aren't you ever afraid, being on duty all night by yourself?" I asked Beth when we checked in.

"Well, we do get a lot of highway drifters and strange people walking through these doors," Beth explained in her slow, southern drawl. "But I'm never afraid. Oh, I'll admit, I used to be. But something happened one morning that changed all that. Now I think of this place as my mission field."

Beth relayed the story about Samuel and the still, small voice she'd heard that cold November morning two years before.

"You never know how someone may take rejection or what they perceive as rejection," she said. "That rejection or apathy could be the last straw for them. We live in a fragile society these days. If I have one goal in life, it's never to be that last straw for anyone."

I understood Beth's reasoning, but I didn't understand the fervency behind her words until she finished her story.

"If you'd been here a month ago, I couldn't have told you any more than what I just shared," she said. Her deep blue eyes danced, and her voice took on a jubilant yet reverent tone. And then she leaned slightly across the front desk as if she were about to reveal a special secret.

"Three weeks ago," Beth began, "about six o'clock one morning, a well-dressed man walked into the lobby, poured himself a cup of coffee, and dropped some money into the honor jar. I was busy and didn't pay much attention to him at first. He lingered for a few minutes at the table and then walked over to the front desk. When I looked up at him, I noticed his eyes looked strangely familiar.

"'Hi, Beth,' he said to me.

"'Do I know you?' I asked curiously.

"'You may not remember me, but I remember you,' the man replied.

"Then he pulled a single yellow rose and a card from the inside of his suit jacket, handed them to me, and left.

"Why, I couldn't imagine who this man was or why he'd brought me a yellow rose! But then I read the letter inside the card."

Beth's eyes were glistening with tears as she reached under the counter for her purse and retrieved a pale yellow envelope with her name printed on it. The front of the card pictured a beautiful bouquet of yellow roses tied with a sky blue ribbon. Inside was a handwritten letter:

Dear Beth,

You may not remember me, but early one morning two years ago, I walked into the lobby of the Yellow Rose. I was tired and so cold that my feet and hands were numb. This was the first motel I'd seen for miles and miles. I'd walked into another one around midnight the night before, but was thrown out and told never to come back. I'm sure they thought I was a bum looking for a handout, but I just needed to rest and get out of the cold for a few minutes. The truth of the matter is that I was on my way to New Mexico to see my father. And I was as discouraged as I've ever been in my life.

You see, a few months before that time, I'd had a bright future ahead of me, with only a year and a half left in medical school. My father had sacrificed for years to pay for my college tuition. Said I had "doctoring" in my blood. His dad was a doctor and hoped his son would follow in his footsteps. But my father admittedly didn't make such good choices in his life. By the time I was almost grown, he realized what a mistake he'd made. So when I showed an interest in becoming a doctor, he encouraged me and raked and scraped to make sure I could fulfill the dream he'd cast aside.

But then he found out he was sick—very sick—and it took every cent he had to pay for his medical bills. It nearly killed him to tell me I'd have to drop out of school for a while. He hoped he'd get better and could keep up the farm and continue raising cattle. But he progressively got worse. I was selfish and could think only of the hours I'd studied to graduate and become a doctor. But my dream was cut short. I quit college. I was despondent, embarrassed, and soon I was out of control emotionally. I knew my father was ill, but I was so angry over having to quit medical school, I didn't even want to see him.

And then the phone call came. Dad only had a few days left to live. My mom had died many years ago, and my only brother had been killed on a construction job when I was still in high school. I was all my father had left. After quitting medical school, I lived with one friend and then another until they all got tired of me mooching off of them. I had no car, no money, and was so depressed no one wanted to hire me.

But something happened inside when I heard my dad was critical. Home was at least twelve hours away by car. But even without a car, I was determined to make it to New Mexico before he died. So I started walking. I hitchhiked twice—something my father told me never to do. A friend had loaned me food money, but it didn't last long. I'm sure my unshaven face and uncombed hair frightened the people inside the motel lobbies and restaurants I ventured into. I learned the harsh truth that appearance does make a difference in the way people treat you. I was so despondent, weary, and cold; I feared I wouldn't make it to my father in time.

Just a few hours before I saw the lights from the Yellow Rose, I voiced a desperate prayer. It went something like this: "Lord, I won't make it if I don't get some help soon. But I'm not even sure You hear me or care. I'm angry and desperate— and I'm about ready to just give up trying to get to New Mexico. If I meet one more heartless person, it'll be the last straw."

When I left the motel lobby that morning with the two sacks you gave me, I knew somehow I'd make it the next few miles to the New Mexico border. You'll never know how those donuts and coffee warmed my heart. I mean this as a compliment—it almost felt like my own mother had given me a care package of love. And even more than the donuts and coffee, the stickers you put on the sacks let me know that God did care and that He'd heard my desperate prayer.

My dad lived ten more days after I arrived home. We grew very close in those last few days. I begged his forgiveness for my ungrateful heart.

And he had just one last request—that I sell the farm and go back to medical school. I'm now a doctor in a town eighty miles from here. I just had to let you know that every day since my "last straw" prayer, I've thanked God for a little corner of heaven called the Yellow Rose and a very special angel named Beth.

Gratefully,

Samuel

There's never a rose in all the world
But makes some green spray sweeter;
There's never a wind in all the sky
But makes some bird wing fleeter;
There's never a star but brings to heaven
Some silver radiance tender;
And never a rosy cloud but helps
To crown the sunset splendor;
No robin but may thrill some heart,
His dawn like gladness voicing;
God gives us all some small sweet way
To set the world rejoicing.

—*Author Unknown*

*W*herever you work or live is truly the mission field where God can use you most. Remember, the people who cross your path are not there by mere coincidence. You never know when one small act of encouragement might be an answer to someone's prayer.

I will send

down showers

in season;

there will be

showers of

blessing.

—Ezekiel 34:26

The course of human history
is determined not by what happens
in the skies, but by
what takes place in our hearts.
—Sir Arthur Keith

Chapter 2

soaking WET AT THE CIRCLE K

The aroma of hot coffee greeted us as we entered the Circle K Café—our favorite spot for breakfast, especially on a cold, rainy Saturday morning. My husband and I joined the long line of customers waiting for a table. Seems we weren't the only ones who'd ventured out in the stormy weather. But the hostess assured us we'd be seated within fifteen minutes.

While I watched the heavy Texas rain pelt against the large, plate-glass windows of the café, my attention was suddenly diverted to a couple running across the parking lot. Neither of them was wearing a raincoat or jacket, and they were drenched and shivering by the time they entered the café.

Their clothes, besides being wet, were ragged and stained. But it was the dented and faded green suitcase the man placed on the foyer floor that really caught my eye. *Why in the world would someone bring a suitcase into a restaurant?* I wondered.

Trying not to stare, I looked around to see if anyone else had noticed the wet couple and their suitcase. But everyone in line seemed involved in typical Saturday-morning chitchat. One couple thumbed through the newspaper, looking for the movie section and discussing their cinema choices. Another couple made a grocery list and talked about rising produce prices. Yet another discussed the day's household chores.

Apparently no one had noticed the dripping, stringy-haired woman and the bedraggled-looking man who were now perched on two stools at the serving counter.

But I couldn't take my eyes off them. I became oblivious to the muffled chatter around me. Even when my husband said something to me, his voice didn't register.

"Earth to Suzie! Honey, are you listening to me?" Harvey asked.

"I'm sorry. I guess not," I confessed.

"What are you thinking about?"

"I'm not really thinking about anything," I said. "I'm watching that couple who just walked in. Did you notice them?"

"What couple?"

"See," I said, gesturing toward the counter, "that couple. I think they're hungry."

"Now, what makes you think that?"

"I don't know," I said, surprised at my own declaration. "I just don't think they have money to order anything."

"Oh, I'm sure they've ordered," Harvey countered. "See, the waitress just gave them some coffee. Their food is probably on the way."

"But they walked in with a suitcase. Don't you think that's strange? I just have a feeling they're hungry!"

Harvey pulled me close to him and smiled. "It's nice that you noticed. But I'm sure they're okay."

I smiled weakly. Whatever had grabbed my heart when that couple walked in and sat down at the counter had also taken over my thoughts and emotions. This wasn't like me—to zero in on strangers in a crowded restaurant. But my soul stirred within me, and my heart pounded as I watched. And waited.

The waitress never served the couple any food.

"I have to talk to them," I whispered to Harvey.

It was as if an unknown force pulled me out of my place in line and ordered my steps to the counter where the strangers slowly sipped their coffee.

What should I say to this couple? If they really were hungry, I didn't want to embarrass or offend them.

Though vividly highlighted to me, it was as if they were invisible to everyone else. A strange compassion engulfed me, and I was close to tears when I asked for some heavenly wisdom and help. "Lord," I prayed silently, "I may be making a fool of myself, but if it's You who have directed my attention to this couple, then give me the words to say to them."

I stepped forward. "Excuse me, sir," I said as calmly as possible. "My husband and I noticed that you came in with a suitcase. It's raining so hard outside, we were wondering if you might need a ride somewhere." (Then my alter ego chided: *Are you out of your mind? What are you thinking?*)

"Well, thank you, ma'am, but we really don't know where we're going yet," the man said.

"Oh. Then can I give you directions? Are you new to the area?"

"Yes, ma'am. Just got here this morning. We're from Mississippi, and I'm hoping to find work here."

"What kind of work do you do?" I asked.

"I'm a painter," he said.

I could hardly believe it. At the time, my husband was a paint contractor and had a crew of men who worked for him.

"Well, what a coincidence!" I replied (although I was certain it wasn't coincidence at all). "My husband just happens to be in that business and might need some help. Have you ordered breakfast yet—or could you join us when we get our table so we can talk?"

Suddenly the man's gray, sullen eyes began to glisten. "Sure, okay," he said, looking at his wife. The whole time she hadn't taken her eyes off her coffee cup.

"My husband will come and get you when our table is ready. It won't be long," I told him as I walked back to the line where Harvey was looking none too pleased with me.

"Honey!" I said excitedly, running my sentences together in order to get it all in before he could ask too many questions. "Guess what? The guy's a painter—and I told him that maybe you could help him with a job— and as soon as we sit down, they're going to join us. See,

21

now when we buy them breakfast, it won't look like charity since we'll be talking about business."

"What's gotten into you?" Harvey objected. "These people could be prison escapees for all you know! Didn't your mother ever tell you not to talk to strangers?"

"I know this isn't like me," I said. "But something's going on inside my heart that I can't explain. I feel compelled to reach out to these people. What can it hurt? We're in a safe place, and the least we can do is buy them breakfast."

"They're probably just transients," Harvey mumbled, beginning to accept defeat.

"Maybe they are. But I believe they're hungry."

"Woman, the things you get me into!"

Soon the waitress ushered us to our table, and Harvey went to meet the strangers. I watched as he shook their hands and escorted them to our table.

Their names were John and Pam. They barely made eye contact with us as they sat down and nervously scooted their chairs close to each other.

"Since this is a business meeting, breakfast is on us. Please order whatever you like," Harvey offered.

I was smiling inside.

When our food came, John and Pam ate as if they

were starved. Come to find out, it had been three days since they'd had a meal. Gently and cautiously we asked them some questions. Why had they left Mississippi? How did they travel to Texas? How long would they be staying? Did they have family here?

"Do you have children?" I asked.

Pam suddenly excused herself and headed toward the restroom.

"We had a child. We lost him in a fire," John explained quietly as a single tear slid down his cheek.

"My wife hasn't been the same since," he continued. "She won't talk to anyone. Her mother wanted to put her in a mental hospital, but I knew that would kill her. Pam's had a hard life and doesn't cope like most people. But she's a good woman. She's just sad. She wanted to leave Mississippi, so we did. We don't have much. Never needed much—just each other and our baby. We hitch-hiked to Louisiana. We slept under a bridge one night, and someone robbed us of what little money we had left. So we walked and then caught another ride. And here we are."

When he finished speaking, John stood up and excused himself.

"I'll be right back," he said.

"Now what?" Harvey said as we sat alone, pondering the story we'd just been told.

"Can you put him to work?" I asked.

"I can, but where will they live in the meantime? We can't take them home. We need to use some wisdom. If we can help them, fine, but let's be sensible."

I agreed. "Let's take them to a hotel for now. It doesn't have to be expensive—just clean. I know we're low on money ourselves, but I have some cash in my purse I'd set aside for a church project. I think this couple needs it more, don't you?"

Once John and Pam returned to the table, we told them our plan. They seemed grateful.

When we got to the hotel, Pam opened her suitcase to retrieve a hairbrush. I noticed that she had packed only two or three dingy items of clothing and a pair of old shoes. We promised we'd return later in the afternoon with supper.

John walked outside the hotel room and shook Harvey's hand. "Can I ask you a question?"

"Sure," Harvey replied.

"Why are you helping us?"

"Well, if we were in your shoes, we hope someone

would help us," Harvey said. "Besides, we believe God wants us to help people whenever we're able."

"But nobody has ever helped us before," John pressed. "Mostly, people have taken from us. I just don't understand."

Harvey patted John's hand. "Just be blessed," he said.

Our hearts were touched by the neediness of this young couple. They'd obviously lived a tragic life, and their future looked dim. How could we possibly make a difference?

When we got home, I called a few friends and told them about Pam and John. They all responded enthusiastically, offering to help with clothing or food. As promised, late that afternoon we returned to the hotel and took some clothes we'd gathered up; two jackets; a small ice chest of milk, cereal, soup, and snacks; a hot plate; and plastic cups, bowls, and utensils—all donations from caring friends. We didn't know what we'd do next, but for the time being they could rest, have some privacy, and eat until they were full.

The next morning Harvey and I went to church as usual. Our Sunday school lesson was from Matthew 25:37–40: "'Lord, when did we see you hungry and feed you, or thirsty and give you something to drink? When did we see you a stranger and invite you in, or needing clothes and clothe you?'… The King will reply, 'I tell you the truth, whatever you did for one of the least of these brothers of mine, you did for me.'"

Our eyes welled with tears, and we asked if we could share John and Pam's story with the class. We explained that we felt humbled that God had placed us in this couple's path to minister to them—to minister to *Him.*

The class discussion then turned to how many times we'd all looked the other way and ignored the tugging in our hearts to get involved in meeting someone's needs.

One man was moved to tears and stood to speak. "God not only allowed you two to find John and Pam, He knew we would be a part of the picture too," he said. "I don't know about the rest of you, but I don't want to miss out on this blessing. I want to help. If anyone wants to join me, I'm passing an envelope around."

Another lady spoke up: "Maybe we can collect enough money to get them out of that hotel and into an apartment. I have a couch, a chair, and bedroom furniture I was planning to put in a garage sale, but I'd like to give them to John and Pam."

By the next morning we'd collected enough money

for one month's rent. Harvey picked up John for work, and several ladies helped me get Pam settled in an apartment. By the end of the day, more people had stepped forward to donate pots and pans, towels, bedding, and even a used stereo and small television.

Pam didn't speak, but she told us "thank you" with her eyes.

John turned out to be one of the most dependable and hard-working employees Harvey ever had. Before long, he was able to buy a car and support his family without our help. All John and Pam had needed was a chance to start over—and people to show they cared. They'd never known God's love before, but as John said more than once, "We know God brought us here, and we know now that there are good people in the world. Our lives will never be the same."

It might be tempting to think it was *our goodness* that prompted Harvey and me to act as earth angels to John and Pam. But it was *God's compassion* that allowed our pathways to cross that day. In all of our busyness, we miss many opportunities to be God's light—to be the vessels that pour out His love. This time, He made sure we opened our eyes.

No, John and Pam didn't encounter good people that

cold, rainy Saturday morning. They encountered God's power within us that longs to be released.

And through John and Pam, we became the *blessed* and *thankful* ones—blessed that we had to wait in line long enough to hear and heed God's summons. And thankful that on at least one rainy, Saturday morning, we were the ones who got soaking wet when God opened the floodgates of heaven and poured out a blessing we could scarcely contain.

In sweet'ning the life of another,
In relieving a brother's distress,
The soul finds its highest advancement
And the noblest blessedness.

The life is alone worth the living
That lives for another's gain;
The life that comes after such living
Is the rainbow after the rain.

—*J. R. Miller*

Wing Tip

Awareness is the first step to being a vessel that God can use. Pay attention to others and take an interest in their needs. Then you, too, can be a catalyst for God's blessings.

And of some

have compassion,

making a difference.

—Jude 1:22 KJV

In the face of men
and women,
I see God.
—Walt Whitman

Chapter 3

A KEY OF compassion

The crisp autumn breeze felt refreshing on Sandy's face as she carried her bag of trash down the sidewalk of her apartment complex. Instead of taking her usual route to the trash bin closest to her building, she spontaneously decided to walk the extra block to the bin located at the opposite end of the complex.

Task completed, Sandy took her time strolling back home in the pleasant evening air. As she rounded a curve, she noticed a well-dressed, professional-looking young woman in the parking lot struggling to open her car door. *Bless her heart*, Sandy whispered to herself, remembering the times she had been locked out of her own car. She, too, had struggled to maneuver a twisted coat hanger through a tiny opening between the window and top of the car door, just as this young woman was doing. Sandy's attempts were never successful, but she reflected gratefully that someone had always come to her rescue.

Instinctively she called from across the parking lot, "Can I help you?"

The distressed young woman turned her head and answered, "I've locked my keys in the car. I can't afford a locksmith, and this wire isn't working!"

"That's happened to me many times," Sandy empathized. "Personally, I've never had any luck opening locked car doors, but I'll sure give it a try if you like."

"Oh, yes. Thank you."

"Do you believe in the power of prayer?" Sandy asked, smiling at the stranger.

"Yes, I do," answered the young woman, her voice quivering.

"Lord, we need to get into this car!" Sandy prayed. "Please help us."

Sandy pried the crooked wire into the doorframe, but

it lodged in one position and wouldn't budge. "I'll be right back," she said finally. "I'm going to get my husband. He'll help us."

Sandy knew that her husband, Lee, had worked many physically exhausting hours that day, so as she walked back to their apartment, she prayed that God would strengthen him and give him a willing heart to help with her mission. When she explained the situation to him, he didn't hesitate to follow her outside.

Sandy and Lee returned to the young woman's little blue car and found her still working tediously with the wire coat hanger.

"Let Lee try," Sandy coaxed. "He can open our van quicker with a coat hanger than he can with a key!"

But no matter what Lee did, the wire wouldn't connect to the inside door latch.

"Do you by chance have another set of keys?" Lee asked the auburn-haired young lady.

"No, I don't."

Lee pulled away from the car door. "This wire is so badly bent, I'm going to the apartment to try to straighten it with a pair of pliers. I'll be back."

"Don't worry," Sandy assured the young woman.

"Lee is good at this. He'll be back soon and have your door unlocked in no time."

But instead of sounding relieved, the young woman's tone and response were unsettling. "You don't understand what is happening here! I need to think—and get a drink of water—in my apartment."

Sandy watched in bewilderment as the woman scurried across the parking lot and into an upstairs apartment. Once again she prayed for God's intervention in helping open the car door.

After several minutes the lady returned, visibly calmer, with a large paper cup filled with water. She sat down on the curb next to Sandy. Her thick, auburn hair cascaded over her violet-blue eyes as she dropped her head and rested her elbows on both knees. "My name is Nancy," she finally spoke.

"Nice to meet you, Nancy. I'm Sandy. Are you all right?"

Nancy didn't answer. Instead she asked, "Why did you offer to help me?"

"Well, you were out here all alone, struggling with your car door, and I know how that feels," Sandy explained. "You just looked like you could use a friend."

Nancy brushed her hair from her face and looked up at Sandy, her eyes now brimming with tears.

"If you need to talk, I'm a pretty good listener," Sandy offered.

Scene after sad scene began unfolding as Nancy confided the story of a life filled with pain and bitter disappointment. The recent betrayal of a dear friend was the last straw for Nancy emotionally.

"This morning I packed all my belongings and took them to my sister's house," Nancy said. "Then, after work, I stopped at a pharmacy and bought all kinds of over-the-counter drugs. I told God on the way home, 'Unless You stop me, I'm going to end my life tonight.' When I parked my car and got out, I realized I'd locked the keys and the drugs inside. My apartment key was in my purse, so I was able to get a coat hanger and try to unlock my car door. That's when you came along. When I stormed off to get a drink of water, I was upset and confused—because suddenly it hit me that God must have sent you to me. He had heard my desperate prayer. If you hadn't come by and offered to help, I probably would have resorted to breaking out the window. And I would have taken those pills by now.

"Do you think God cares about me that much—that He would have you come by just in time to save my life?"

Sandy's own tears flowed freely as she pulled Nancy close and cradled her in her arms. In the stillness of that sacred moment, no words were needed.

Within the hour, Sandy and Nancy heard the gentle clicking of the lock on Nancy's car door. At last, Lee was successful.

Nancy walked over to her car, reached beneath the driver's seat, and pulled out a brown paper bag. "Here," she said, handing it to Sandy. "I don't need what's in here anymore. I have no more doubts that God is real and that He sent you here tonight. Thank you for listening—and caring—and showing me that He has a plan for my life."

Divine delays are often the unseen hand of God working in our midst. It's no mystery now why Lee—who had always been an accomplished amateur locksmith—was unable to open Nancy's car door immediately.

And it was God who had changed Sandy's routine and led her to the side of one who was crying out to Him. While Lee worked on unlocking Nancy's car door, God used the key of Sandy's compassion to unlock the door of Nancy's heart.

God, the great Locksmith of heaven and earth, holds the keys to every heart.

And He uses earthly vessels—men and women who house His very nature and divine power—to turn those keys and unlock the doors that separate wounded hearts from His unchanging love.

The happiest heart that ever beat
Was in some quiet breast
That found the common daylight sweet
And left to heaven the rest.

—John Vance Cheney

Wing Tip

$\mathcal{B}$e alert to your surroundings each day. God works miracles in the most ordinary moments. Any day or any hour, He may use you as His ambassador of compassion to unlock a heart that is filled with hopelessness and pain.

Our mouths were filled

with laughter,

our tongues

with songs of joy.

Then it was said

among the nations,

"The LORD has done

great things for them."

—Psalm 126:2

I believe that imagination is stronger than knowledge—
That myth is more potent than history.
I believe that dreams are more powerful than fact—
That hope always triumphs over experience—
That laughter is the only cure for grief.
I believe that love is stronger than death.
                                    —Robert Fulghum

Chapter 4

LOVE IN A **bear** SUIT

The saying is true: A picture *is* worth a thousand words. The surprised look on Joanna's face, followed by a smile as wide as Texas, can only be described as indescribable.

She had no idea when she opened her front door that night what was about to take place.

Nor did I.

Earlier in the day, Joanna had called me with bad news. She'd been to the doctor, and her latest test results showed the cancer she'd been battling for more than a year was still raging. The chemotherapy and radiation had done little to hold it at bay. For the first time since her diagnosis, I

43

heard—through sobs and broken sentences—hopelessness and fear in my dear friend's voice. Until now, she'd been full of faith and high spirits.

But today was different.

I prayed with her before we hung up, but afterward, I cried. Slow, silent tears.

"How can I help Joanna, Lord?" I prayed in desperation. "How can I encourage her, minister to her, give her hope? Please show me what to do."

I called two other close friends—Janice and Brenda. With Joanna, we were the "Steel Magnolias." That's what Joanna's husband, Robert, called us, explaining that our friendship reminded him of the friends in the popular 1989 movie. The four of us live an hour apart in opposite directions and don't get together all that often, but we stay in touch, praying for each other and pulling together when there is a need.

"Janice, have you talked to Joanna yet?" I asked.

"Yes, we just hung up," Janice said.

"Do you plan on going to see her tonight?"

"Yes. I was thinking about taking supper over there for her and Robert. If you and Harvey come, I'll get my Charlie to come too. I'll bring enough food for everybody. When you call Brenda, tell her not to eat before-hand if she can join us."

"Okay," I agreed. "I'll call Brenda at work in a few minutes. I keep feeling that we need to do something really special for Joanna—something different—to lift her spirits. I know we can go and visit, pray, and take them supper, but how can we make Joanna smile again?"

"I don't know," Janice replied. "But let me know if you think of something."

I waited before I called Brenda to tell her the plans, hoping God would give me an idea. *What will make Joanna smile?*

From out of the blue, a wild idea formed in my mind.

"Lord, surely this isn't You planting this kind of thought in my head! I know You work in mysterious ways, but I'll have to pray about this some more!" I said out loud.

But the thoughts and ideas continued to flow—so much so that I finally dialed Brenda's work number to run my idea by her.

Her response didn't surprise me.

"You're going to do *what?* Are you sure this idea is the Lord's doing?" she laughed.

"Well, I *think* it is," I said. "I know it sounds crazy. I thought so too. But I can't get away from thinking about what it might do for Joanna."

"But, Susan—a *bear suit?* You've got to be kidding! Where in the world could you even find one to rent?"

"Well…I was thinking you could help me out since I'm here in the boonies and you're in the big city of Dallas."

"Oh, please!" Brenda objected. "I can't find you a bear suit. I've got work to do! Besides, who would I call?"

"A costume shop. Just ask if they have a teddy bear suit for rent," I coaxed. "As wild as it seems, I think this is divinely inspired! Joanna needs something special—a memory she'll never forget—to let her know we love her so much we'd do almost anything to make her laugh again. Tell me you don't think I'm crazy!"

"You're crazy!" Brenda laughed.

"I knew you'd say that! But can't you see it? We'll have a theme. I've already called Harvey on his cell phone to ask him to find the Elvis tape with the old song 'Let Me Be Your Teddy Bear.'"

"Okay, *if* I can find you a bear suit to wear, and Janice brings the food, what should I do?" Brenda asked.

"How about getting Joanna a cuddly teddy bear and some colorful balloons?" I suggested.

"That sounds good. Let me see if I can find this bear suit, and I'll call you back."

Thirty minutes later my phone rang. It was Brenda.

"I can't find a bear suit anywhere in Dallas," she said. "I've found gorilla suits, rabbit and dog suits, but no bear suits! So now what? Are you sure this is a God thing?"

"Well, I guess we'll know soon enough," I responded. "If there's no bear costume in Dallas, I'm sure there's nothing out here in the boonies. But I'll try the surrounding towns."

I pulled out the phone book with listings from several adjacent counties and searched the yellow pages under C for a costume shop within thirty miles. Lo and behold, I found one in my very own town!

I quickly dialed the number, praying that I wasn't totally off my rocker and that this was the answer to my prayer.

"Hello," I said. "I was wondering if you might by chance have a bear suit."

"Well, as a matter of fact, we do," the shopkeeper answered without hesitation.

I was so shocked, I asked again. "You do? You *really do* have a bear suit—not Smokey the Bear or a grizzly bear, but a *teddy bear* suit?"

"Yes ma'am, we surely do."

"What is your overnight rental fee?" I asked, still incredulous.

"One hundred and twenty-five dollars," the shopkeeper said.

"You're kidding, right? I don't want to buy it—just rent it for a few hours."

"That's our rental fee," the woman answered firmly.

Now what? I thought. *I can't afford to spend that much! Even if the girls went in with me, that's still a lot of money just to wear a bear suit for thirty minutes.*

My heart sank. "I'll have to get back with you," I told the lady on the phone. "I really wanted to do something special for a friend who's going through a very tough time, but this is way out of my budget."

I was about to hang up when the woman began to ask me a few questions about Joanna. "I can tell you're disappointed about this bear suit," she said finally. "And I've never done this for anyone before, but how about renting the suit for half the price I quoted you?"

"Oh my! Are you sure? This will be such a blessing to

my friend," I gushed. "Thank you so much! I'll pick it up within the hour." I wanted to leap like a kid when I got off the phone—and I couldn't wait to call Brenda back.

"You're never going to believe where I found a bear suit!" I shouted. "Practically in my own backyard. See, this must be God!"

We both laughed as we finalized our plans for the evening. We'd meet at Joanna's house at six-thirty. I'd have my portable cassette player in hand, cued to start playing Elvis's "Let Me Be Your Teddy Bear" when Joanna answered the door. Brenda would bring the balloons and toy teddy bear with a card from all of us. Janice would bring the food.

Once we arrived, Harvey had to help me out of the car because the huge, furry bear head almost filled the entire front seat. He put our dog's leash around my neck so he could lead me up to the house.

Everyone converged on Joanna's front porch. Charlie, Janice, and her cousin Susie carried armloads of food in containers; Brenda was partially hidden behind a mass of purple and yellow balloons; and Harvey had his hands full trying to keep me from tripping over my twenty-four-inch bear paws.

We rang the doorbell. Silently, I prayed we were doing the right thing.

Joanna turned the doorknob.

Elvis started singing!

I grabbed Joanna's hand, and we jitterbugged around the room. She giggled like a child and fell onto the couch laughing and holding her sides. When she regained her composure, she read the friendship card and a poem I'd written for her called "Tough Bear."

As she hugged the plush teddy bear Brenda had brought, the tears came.

"Y'all are too much!" she cried. "I can't believe you did all this for me. I could never forget this in a million years. I don't know when I've laughed so hard."

That night we feasted, prayed together, and embraced God's gift of laughter. As someone once said, "Laughter is the closet thing to the grace of God." God Himself says in Proverbs 17:22 that laughter is like medicine.

Yes, a picture really is worth a thousand words. And if, through the pain and adversities of this life, our hearts can remember the portraits of laughter we've shared with friends, we'll have been given a precious gift: a glimpse of heaven here on earth.

Tough Bear

I'm a tough bear, can't you see?
I'm strong enough for
both you and me!
Hold on to me when you're
alone in the night,
And don't ever worry
'bout squeezing too tight!
'Cause I've been sent to bring
comfort and cheer,
And tell you you're loved
because you're so dear.

—Susan Duke

Wing Tip

*D*on't be afraid to be creative and spontaneous and to go the extra mile to make someone smile. When you make memories for others, you also make them for yourself—memories that live forever in the photo album of your heart.

I will sing

of your strength,

in the morning

I will sing of your love;

for you are my fortress, my

refuge in times

of trouble.

—Psalm 59:16

All I have seen

teaches me to trust

the Creator for all

I have not seen.

—Ralph Waldo Emerson

Chapter 5

HIGHWAY TO heaven

Already running late for her career-training class, Allie waited impatiently at the intersection for the red light to turn green. But the shrill sound of screeching tires behind her forewarned that she was about to be rear-ended. Within seconds, a small red pickup slammed into the back of her little silver Mazda, pushing it several feet forward. Allie sat, stunned and shaking, waiting for the driver who had just plowed into her to emerge from his truck.

The balding, middle-aged man calmly walked around Allie's car, evaluating the damage. Seeing that it was relatively minor, he walked to the driver's side of Allie's car and almost jovially quipped, "Well, young lady, it looks as if you're having a bad day."

"No, sir. I'm having a bad life!" Allie sharply retorted.

The sound of her own words resonated like a clanging alarm bell in her soul—the final jolt to her already fragile emotions. Right then and there Allie made a decision.

In the midst of struggling to keep her three-year marriage from falling apart and enrolling in a career-training school, she had received news that her mother had been diagnosed with pancreatic cancer. Torn between going to be with her mother and staying to work on her marriage and career, she had become so stressed out she could barely manage a clear thought.

That morning, metal slamming into metal appeared insignificant compared to the collision of feelings that struck Allie's heart.

Immediately she knew: Her mother needed her—and she needed her mother.

Allie hastily scribbled her phone number on a scrap of paper, gave it to the other driver, and made a U-turn in the middle of the street. She drove home, packed her suitcase, called her husband, and told him she was leaving for the East Coast to be with her mom.

Allie felt weak and vulnerable as she loaded her car,

buckled her seatbelt, and pulled out of her driveway. Having never driven a long distance alone, she lacked confidence that she could actually make the long drive ahead of her—not just physically, but emotionally. She didn't consider herself a very religious person, but just before she turned onto the freeway, she paused and did something she hadn't done in a long time: She prayed, asking God to help her safely drive the twelve hours to her mother's house.

Allie had never used the citizen-band radio her husband had installed in her car some time before, but she decided to turn it on—just for a sense of security. About ten miles into the trip, the CB crackled, and a deep, raspy voice said, "What's your handle, Missy? You in the silver Mazda."

The unexpected voice startled Allie, and she wasn't sure if she should respond.

"Handle?" Allie said clumsily as she pressed the microphone button.

"Yes, ma'am. You know, your handle—your CB name."

"Well, my name is Allie, but I don't really know how to use one of these. Who are you?"

"I'm Ol' Eagle Eyes," the voice responded. "I guess

57

we'll just call you Allie Cat. How's that? I noticed you're drivin' mighty fast, Missy. Maybe you best slow down a bit so you'll get to wherever it is you're goin'. Is anything wrong?"

Allie's voice quivered as she told Ol' Eagle Eyes where she was headed and why she was in such a hurry.

"Well, Miss Allie Cat, I know the good Lord wants you to get to your mother's house safe and sound, so you just run behind me, and I'll make sure your speed stays steady. And just so you know, I'm a pretty good listener if you need to talk. Sometimes it helps."

The raspy voice took on a quality of gentle concern and compassion.

For well over a hundred miles, Allie Cat and Ol' Eagle Eyes talked. Occasionally, he'd quote a scripture about hope or encouragement. Allie felt a strange sense of peace and was amazed at how quickly the time passed.

Finally, Ol' Eagle Eyes told Allie it was time for him to exit the freeway.

"You be careful now, Allie Cat. I'll be prayin' for ya, Missy," he said as he steered his big orange truck onto the exit ramp.

Feelings of sadness and vulnerability emerged again as

Allie watched the eighteen-wheeler pull off the freeway. But within moments, another voice came across the CB.

"Got your ears on, Allie Cat?"

"I thought you got off at the last exit," Allie responded, thinking Ol' Eagle Eyes must still be within talking range.

"I'm Tender Heart," the voice said. "I'm takin' over for Eagle Eyes. He said to make sure you keep your speed down and your courage up! Just stay behind me, Missy, and you'll be fine."

Allie spotted a dark blue eighteen-wheeler just ahead. She eased over into the right lane and caught up with Tender Heart, staying a safe distance behind the big diesel.

Tender Heart was just that—tender-hearted. Allie didn't have to retell her story about her mother. He already knew, compliments of Ol' Eagle Eyes. He talked about his own mom and how she had overcome cancer a few years before. "It's tough, but with enough love around her, your mom can get through it," he assured Allie.

Several more miles down the road, Tender Heart made his exit. Allie stopped to eat and stretch her legs, reflecting on the amazing compassion of two strangers toward someone they didn't know. When she crawled back into her little silver car, she braced herself to spend the rest of the trip alone.

Allie pulled back onto the freeway and turned on her car radio, hoping to find a clear station to help keep her awake for the last few hundred miles. But her attempts were futile, finding instead only static. She switched the CB back on but figured no one would be talking in the wee hours of the morning. She was determined to get to her mom's house by the time the sun came up.

About twenty minutes had passed when a voice rattled across the CB speaker.

"Allie Cat! You out there anywhere? I've been trying to find ya. Tender Heart said for me to take over for him. You can call me Soul Man."

Allie quickly grabbed the microphone. "I'm here, Soul Man!" she said. "Where are you?"

He gave her a mile marker, and within minutes she spotted a yellow cab with an empty flatbed.

"Just run behind me, Allie Cat," Soul Man said. "We're gonna get you to your mama's."

A single, grateful tear trickled slowly down Allie's cheek.

Soul Man was a singer with a definite African-American accent. He offered up his own bluesy rendition of "Rock of Ages," a few musings from his childhood, and a huge helping of encouragement to Allie—reassuring her that God would bless her efforts to comfort her mother. Then he, too, made his exit from the freeway.

Only a hundred and sixty miles to go, Allie thought. *Surely I can make it now.* But Allie's eyelids felt like lead weights. *If only Soul Man could have stayed with me a few more miles.*

Allie was beginning to think she might have to pull over and sleep for a while—something she definitely didn't feel comfortable doing. Then out of the blue came another voice over the CB.

"Allie Cat. Come in, Allie Cat. Are you all right?"

"Yes, I'm all right!" Allie laughed. "Are you taking over for Soul Man?"

"Yes ma'am! I'll be with ya the rest of the way."

Allie wasn't as talkative this last part of her journey, but she listened as the voice over the CB spoke softly about relationships between parents and children, priorities, and the true meaning of life. Allie could tell this person had a real relationship with God, and she even told him she envied his faith and outlook on life.

Before long Allie realized she was only seven miles from the exit leading to her mother's home. "It's almost time for me to turn off. How can I ever thank you for helping me these last few miles?" Allie asked her traveling companion.

"No thanks necessary, ma'am. You just go and love your mother and remember that God loves you both."

Once again, Allie's tears surfaced. And then she remembered something.

"Hey! I never got your name—or rather, your handle. What is it?"

"Angel, ma'am."

Before Allie could say good-bye to Angel, static overtook the airwaves.

It was time for Allie to exit.

Just as the golden morning sun peeked above the horizon, Allie turned into her mother's driveway. A deep periwinkle sky, awash with amethyst and crimson swirls, bespoke her soul's silent praise.

Allie crawled slowly out of her car, took off her shoes, and stood barefoot on the damp emerald grass of her mother's front yard. In the stillness of that sacred moment, she lifted her eyes, stretched her arms heavenward, and spoke out loud: "Thank You, God, for answering my prayer. Thank You for my mother, my marriage, and my life. And Lord, on this beautifully divine morning, thank You for my highway angels who showed me that the road to heaven is paved with Your love."

All the way my Savior leads me—
What have I to ask beside?
Can I doubt his tender mercy,
Who through life has been my guide?

—*Fanny J. Crosby*

God promises that He will never leave you or forsake you. You never need to fear the unknown, for along life's highways, He commissions heavenly angels—and often earth angels—to offer assistance and help guide you through difficult circumstances.

God does speak—

now one way, now another—

though man may not perceive it.

In a dream, in a vision of the night,

when deep sleep falls on men

as they slumber in their beds.

—Job 33:14–15

There are only two ways to live your life.

One is as though nothing is a miracle.

The other as though everything is a miracle.

—Albert Einstein

Chapter 6

touched BY AN ANGEL'S prayer

By nightfall I had succumbed to the despair in my heart. One more day and one more obstacle had finally brought me to the edge of giving up.

I'd stood on every Bible promise I could find, believing that any day God would send the breakthrough our family needed to finally see daylight in our financial crisis. But a series of disasters continued to plague us, bringing us to our knees in more ways than one. It was the mid-eighties, and my husband had lost his business due to the big savings-and-loan crash—just as we were in the middle of building a house in the country. Construction—and life itself, it seemed—had come to a halt.

A sort of weakness unlike any I'd ever felt before seemed to settle in my soul, and a sense of hopelessness replaced my normally optimistic temperament. I wasn't even sure I knew how to pray anymore. As I slid into bed that night, I pulled the covers up around my shoulders and prayed the only prayer left in my heart: "Lord, just give me strength for one more day. If it's possible, pour it into me while I sleep tonight, because I don't think I can take one more day of disappointment. I admit that my faith is weak right now, so all I'm asking is for strength. Amen."

I barely remember finishing that short prayer before I was sleeping soundly and dreaming—a most unusual dream. In the dream I was sitting at a table in a large room with a group of women. A tall man walked up to our table, crooked his elbow, and held out his arm in a gentlemanly fashion, as if to escort someone. I could tell he was waiting for one of us to take his arm. But when I looked around the table to see which of the women he was waiting for, I realized that no one saw him but me.

Immediately I knew I was supposed to stand up and take his arm. I did, and he began to escort me across the room. As we were walking, I looked up into his face and noticed that he bore an uncanny resemblance to an elderly deacon in my church whom I dearly loved!

Suddenly the man let go of my arm and stood directly in front of me. He spoke my name: "Susan." At that moment I somehow perceived that he was an angel. His voice rumbled with a gentle authority as he held up his right hand and instructed me to do the same. Without hesitation, I did as I was told. "Susan," he repeated, "God has sent me to tell you that He has you in His *right hand.*"

The dream ended.

As sunlight streamed through my bedroom window the next morning, I found myself wanting to stay asleep and remember every detail of my dream. But as my sleepy eyes opened, I was immediately aware that the tension and worry that had been my constant companions each day for months were gone. Instead of dread, my heart was filled with peace. I had a strange sense that this had been no ordinary dream. Whatever it meant, it had gotten my attention. I rolled over to shake my husband. "Honey, wake up," I whispered. "I need to ask you something."

Without opening his eyes, Harvey groaned, "What? What's so important at this hour of the morning?"

"What exactly does the *right hand* of God mean?" I asked.

Being an avid Bible scholar, he answered without a pause. "It denotes a place of strength—and of honor and favor."

When he said "strength," that was all I needed to hear. God had answered my prayer. He really had poured strength into me while I slept! Was it possible that He had actually sent an angelic messenger to assure me that He had heard my faint and desperate cry?

That morning I felt more strength and hope than I'd felt in a long time. Nothing had changed. No miracle had occurred in our physical circumstances, but something was different inside of me. It was as if God Himself had wrapped His arms around me, and in the shelter of His loving arms, I felt safe and secure. He knew my name. He knew our needs. His presence was enough.

But this is not the end of the story. It could have been. If nothing else had happened, it still would have been an extraordinary moment that I would have held in my heart forever. But the best was yet to come.

The following Sunday at church, after the conclusion of the morning service, I walked into the church kitchen to get a drink of water. There was sweet Mr.

Hoyle, the elderly gentleman whom the angel in my dream resembled.

"Well, hello, Miss Suzie," he said, smiling. "How are you doing today?"

"I'm fine, Mr. Hoyle," I answered as I patted him on the back. He reached over and hugged me, and before I realized what I was saying, I quipped, "You know, I think you must be my guardian angel."

He chuckled warmly and replied, "Well, Suzie, I'd love to be your guardian angel."

I never intended to tell anyone but my husband about my dream for fear that it would sound far-fetched. But I didn't want Mr. Hoyle to think I was being flippant or silly, so I began to explain.

"I know you're not really my guardian angel, Mr. Hoyle, but I did have a dream about an angel that resembled you," I said. "I don't mean this disrespectfully, but he looked like a much younger, stronger version of you." Then I shared the whole dream with Mr. Hoyle and concluded, "I can't help but wonder why the angel looked like you."

For a moment Mr. Hoyle seemed to be pondering my question as he looked down at the floor. Then, ever so slowly, he began to raise his head, and I saw tears brimming in his twinkling blue eyes. When our eyes met, he spoke in almost a whisper, "Suzie, I think I know why that angel looked like me."

"You do?" I asked with surprise.

He reached into his pants pocket and pulled out a small, wrinkled scrap of white paper. "Do you know what's on this paper?" Mr. Hoyle asked.

"Why, no, I don't," I replied.

As he opened it and held it up, I could hardly believe my eyes.

"It says...*Suzie*," Mr. Hoyle continued.

I was puzzled. "But why? I don't understand."

"Do you remember about six months ago when we drew names at the Christmas banquet? We were supposed to pray for that person during the week of Christmas. Well, I drew your name. I put that piece of paper in my pocket, right along with my change, so I'd be sure to remember to pray every day. When the week was over, I started to throw the paper away, but I just couldn't do it. I kept it, and it's been in my pocket ever since. So, you see, several times each day, whenever I reach into my pocket and feel that little piece of paper, I pray for Suzie. And one thing I always pray is for God to give you *strength*."

Now I was the one with tears streaming down my face. I hugged my earth angel and thanked him for standing in the gap for me each day. He assured me he wouldn't throw the piece of paper away but would continue to pray for me.

My dream and Mr. Hoyle will always be reminders to me that even when we feel too weak to pray for ourselves, someone in God's family is standing in the gap, praying and petitioning the Father on our behalf. That's the kind of bond God intended for His children to have. And God is the kind of Father who just might send an angel to give us a message of hope—sometimes disguised as an ordinary man who believes in the power of prayer.

The Unseen Bridge

There is a bridge whereof the span
Is hidden in the heart of man,
And reaches, without pile or rod,
Into the plentitude of God.

It carries all that honestly
Is faith or hope or charity.
No other traffic will it bear:
This broad yet narrow Bridge of Prayer.

—*Gilbert Thomas*

*N*ever underestimate the power of your prayers, however weak they may seem. God hears your cries and can place your burden into the interceding heart of someone who will touch heaven on your behalf. Be diligent to be that bridge of prayer for others when God brings them to mind.

The LORD is good,

a refuge

in times of trouble.

He cares for those

who trust in him.

—Nahum 1:7

To love for the sake of being loved is human,

but to love for the sake of loving is angelic.

—Alphonse De Lamartine

Chapter 7

MAJOR **memo**

The morning sunlight streamed through Jackie's bedroom window, gently nudging her from a restless sleep. She covered her eyes with her crumpled blue pillow, seeking a few more moments of respite from the daylight's dismal reality.

Jackie had stopped hoping for better tomorrows some time ago. With each new sunrise she merely wondered how she, her three small children, and the new life she was carrying inside her would survive.

The faint ringing of her doorbell finally succeeded in fully waking her.

Who could be at my door this early in the morning? Jackie wondered as she gathered her faded pink robe around her and went to see who was there.

"Yes?" she said, barely cracking the door as she peered out at the tiny woman in thick eyeglasses standing on her steps. The woman's gray hair was twisted neatly in a bun beneath a hat that appeared to be part of the navy-colored uniform she was wearing.

"I'm Major Saunders—Margaret's mother."

Jackie and Margaret had been friends in junior high, and the two young women had recently rekindled their friendship. Jackie had never met Margaret's mother in person. She'd only heard her firm-sounding voice a few times on the telephone. *The big voice,* Jackie thought, *certainly doesn't match the gentle face on my doorstep.*

"Margaret is worried about you," the petite woman continued.

Casting her eyes downward, Jackie hesitantly responded, "So am I."

"Well, I've come to take you home with me. To live."

"But, Mrs.—I mean, Major Saunders," Jackie stuttered, "I have three small children and another one on the way. I couldn't possibly come live with you."

"I'll not take no for an answer, child," the little woman stated firmly. "Now you pack your things and your children's things too. I'll be back to get you this afternoon."

Jackie was at a loss for words. The truth was, Jackie had never had the privilege of saying much of anything about what she wanted or didn't want. Her soul was calloused and scarred from years of emotional abuse and neglect dating back to her childhood. Married when she was practically a child herself, Jackie had become entrapped in a downward spiral of more abuse that at last all but crippled her emotionally. Even though she'd taken a job as a waitress to try to support herself and her children, there was never enough money to make ends meet.

Jackie reluctantly but gratefully accepted the kind offer from Margaret's mother. What else could she do in her precarious situation? Once everything was loaded into Major Saunders's car, Jackie's little family began their journey across town. The first time Jackie saw the big white clapboard house where she and her children would be living, she felt a strange stirring inside—as if she'd come home from a long trip. The old house, while unfamiliar to her, seemed to open invisible arms, beckoning her and her babies inside.

A huge hallway separated two distinct living quarters on either side. "I think you'll have plenty of room here. Just consider this part of the house your own," Major Saunders said, pointing to the left.

"Now, there's only one thing we need to get out of the way," she continued. "For a very select few, I'm known as 'Memo.' And that's what I want you and these lovely children to call me: Memo."

In that moment, Jackie felt warm, safe, and welcome—perhaps for the first time in her life. She'd never experienced real love. Not like other people. The simple words of affirmation and kindness that children naturally crave from their parents never came for Jackie. There were no family picnics or Sunday morning church services—only constant berating from an unstable mother who made it clear Jackie was not wanted.

Memo, a major in the Salvation Army, understood something of what Jackie felt. Memo had been abandoned by her mother at age thirteen and left at the Salvation Army, which literally became her family and her life's work. She never married, but that didn't stop her from experiencing the fullness of motherhood.

When a frail baby girl with terrible physical problems was left on the doorstep of the Salvation Army storefront, Major Margaret Saunders broke the rules and even risked losing her rank to take the baby in. She named the baby Margaret after herself, found doctors who could treat her paralysis, and adopted the little girl no one wanted—the little girl who would one day become Jackie's friend. By the time little Margaret was two years old, she was fine. Proper medical treatment and Memo's care had healed her.

Major Memo was less than five feet tall, but she had a heart as big as the sky—a heart that led her to adopt a son and a daughter and help raise many other children through the years. She was also a praying woman. Jackie soon learned that when Memo's door was closed, she was down on her knees in prayer, petitioning the Father on behalf of Jackie and her children. Those prayers gave Jackie a sense of spiritual covering and wrapped her in more love than she'd felt in a lifetime. Beyond providing a place of refuge, sharing God's Word, and introducing Jackie and her children to church, Memo "literally loved me to Jesus," Jackie says today.

Memo never preached or offered advice. Over many cups of hot tea, she simply listened patiently, answered questions, and sweetly assured Jackie that she was special and loved. Jackie didn't realize at the time that Memo was planting seeds in her fragile life that would flourish and establish her in a lifelong relationship with God. More than food and a haven in the midst of a storm, Memo gave Jackie the gift of a spiritual heritage—a deep and abiding faith that has been an anchor in Jackie's life and the lives of her children and grandchildren for many years.

One of Jackie's most cherished memories of Memo took place after the birth of her fourth child. When she returned to Memo's house from the hospital, new baby in tow, there was Memo—standing on the front porch with a smile as bright as sunshine, looking much younger than her eighty-something years, waiting with outstretched arms to welcome another baby home.

Someone has said that every time a bell rings, an angel is getting wings. Jackie can confirm that it's true. The woman who rang Jackie's doorbell that spring morning so many years ago may have *looked* like a little gray-haired lady in a navy uniform, but Jackie knows it was an angel who gave her the marching orders that saved her family that day and for generations to come.

Salvation Army bells still ring here on earth, and Jackie can't help but remember her angel every time she hears one. Major Memo is probably ringing a few bells of her own in heaven—and rejoicing that the earthly prayers she once prayed for Jackie are still being answered. Memo knew the secret of serving: that we're really all in the same army, no matter the label. And God, the great Commander of Love, uses majors and Memos to rescue His children from life's storms.

It may be little we can do
To help another, it is true;
But better is a little spark
Of kindness when the way is dark,
Than one should miss the road to heaven
For lack of light we might have given.

—*Anonymous*

Wing Tip

*Y*ou may just have the cup of nourishment, shelter, or hope that someone needs today. Be ready to pour out God's love on those He places in your path. When you share God's blessings, you give an eternal heritage of everlasting love.

A cheerful heart

is good medicine.

—Proverbs 17:22

Always laugh when you can;

it is a cheap medicine.

Merriment is a philosophy

not well understood.

It is the sunny side of existence.

—Lord Byron

Chapter 8

nurse DUCKY AND THE HA HA team

"Hello, is this Marcy Graves?"

"Yes," Marcy answered, not recognizing the voice on the other end of her office phone.

"This is Dr. Patch Adams."

Marcy frowned. "Mark, honey, if you're playing a joke, I really don't have time to talk to you right now. I have to take care of my patients," she said.

"No, no, this isn't Mark. It really is Dr. Patch Adams."

"Sure it is," Marcy shot back, obviously miffed at the joke she thought her husband was playing on her. "I'm telling you, I don't have time for this. I have patients and lots of work to do!"

As the Director of Cardiopulmonary Neurodiagnostics at Harris Methodist Southwest Hospital in Fort Worth, Texas, Marcy had been greatly inspired by the movie *Patch Adams,* the real-life story of a doctor who uses humor to relate to his patients. She figured it would be just like her husband, Mark, an avid practical joker, to call her at work and pretend to be the famous doctor.

"Well, don't you have Caller ID?" the insistent man on the phone continued.

"No, I don't have Caller ID," Marcy replied.

"Well, how about a fax machine?"

"Yes, yes, you *know* I have a fax machine."

"Well, can you give me your fax number?"

Marcy decided to give in and go along with her husband's little game. She told him the fax number, hung up, and casually strolled to the fax machine. *Mark is certainly going to a lot of trouble for his little joke*, she thought.

Her frustration with her husband continued to mount—until she grabbed the piece of paper from the fax machine and read the message and its source. It was from Gesundheit Institute in West Virginia, the hospital founded by the *real* Patch Adams!

Mortified, she quickly dialed the number on the faxed memo.

"Dr. Adams, I'm so sorry!" she gushed when the doctor answered.

Graciously, Dr. Adams explained that he was putting together a group from America to go to China on an "Ambassadors of Love and Caring" tour.

"Would you like to go?" he asked.

Marcy could hardly believe her beet-red-from-embarrassment ears.

"Well, of course, I want to go! Count me in!"

The trip was a dream come true for Marcy. After watching *Patch Adams*, she had begun incorporating humor in the medical care she'd been giving patients for more than twenty years. Like the famous doctor, she knew that treating the whole person—body, mind, and spirit—makes all the difference in healing.

Feeling inspired, she had approached the administrators at Harris Methodist Hospital about starting a clown troupe program for hospital patients.

Their first question was direct: "How much will it cost?"

"Nothing," Marcy answered.

"Then let's do it!" they said.

Marcy had sent out flyers to hospital employees to see if anyone was interested in participating. She was thrilled when people from radiology, nursing, respiratory therapy, medical records, and medical affairs responded eagerly. She gathered costumes and props and called the first meeting of the *Ha HaS* (*Healing and Humor at Southwest*).

Now every Wednesday afternoon a team of highly intelligent medical professionals gathers in her office to transform themselves into gleeful and amusing clowns. Marcy magically becomes Nurse Ducky, donning an old-fashioned nurse's uniform, a bulging red nose, an oversized nurse's hat, and three-inch-long eyelashes embellished with rhinestones. Her sidekick, a duck puppet named Quackers, dresses just like Nurse Ducky and flirts with all the male patients.

Other characters include Dr. Cat Scan, who dresses as a cat and carries a huge magnifying glass; Photo Kitty, who takes pictures of patients (actually exaggerated cartoon caricatures that Marcy draws); and Smiley Bubbles, who blows bubbles into every room and seems to make older patients especially happy! The troupe also includes

Dr. Feel-Good; the Health and Healing Fairy; and Dee, a former patient who wears heart-shaped eyeglasses and juggles very badly. (When Dee was seriously ill, she declared that if she recovered she would join this team of joyful earth angels whose laughter had helped her so much!)

From three o'clock until four-thirty on Wednesdays, the Ha HaS visit patients of all ages from the fourth floor down to the emergency room. They pass out "mirth-aid kits" that include whistles for patients to call the floor nurses (they just *love* that!) and little plastic bottles labeled "Prescription for a happy day—take one daily or as needed." Inside each bottle are funny sayings and encouraging Bible verses written on slips of paper.

There is one place the Ha HaS won't go, however. "We never—I repeat, *never*—visit women in labor," Marcy laughs. "They are not in the mood for humor! I've had the hair literally pulled off my arms!"

When hospital administrators saw the positive way patients were responding to the clown troupe, they asked Marcy to do a study to prove that humor offered more than just fun and amusement—that it actually helped sick people get well. So Marcy's team tested a group of pneumonia patients who were approximately the same age. The group was treated first with normal nursing and respiratory services, and their progress status was recorded. Then humor was incorporated into their care, and their progress was recorded once again. The study showed that patients who received humor along with their normal care had a decrease in heart rate of twenty beats per minute; a decrease in respiratory rate; a twenty percent drop in blood pressure; and a decrease in serum cortisol, which normally rises when a person is stressed.

Marcy not only compiled and recorded the report, but also had it published in a couple of medical magazines. She even presented it to the 1999 International Respiratory Care Congress. When Patch Adams read Marcy's report, he called her and invited her to go to China.

Marcy learned much during her sixteen-day trip with Dr. Adams's team of "goodwill ambassadors"—doctors, nurses, respiratory therapists, and even a few professional clowns. They all met in Los Angeles and then flew to Hong Kong, Shanghai, Beijing, and Nanjing, where they visited hospitals, orphanages, and hospices.

"We just spread love and joy to everyone we met," Marcy says. "The people in China didn't understand what was being said, but they understood that we were there to make them smile. Humor transcends language, culture barriers, and all differences. Humor is for everyone."

At one orphanage, Marcy made her way into a back room that was supposed to be off-limits to visitors. "I found a tiny baby girl with a condition that is like water on the brain," she remembers. "I felt so grieved when I found out she probably wouldn't live more than six weeks. They don't name orphans over there, so I scooped her up like a mother cat, hugged and kissed her, and named her Constance Beaverhausen because I thought she needed an important-sounding name. I spent the better part of an hour singing hymns, Christmas songs, and anything else I could think of. I prayed over her and promised her that whatever happened, I would always think of her and try to help someone like her."

When Marcy returned to the United States, she fulfilled her promise to the little girl by getting in touch with Dr. Chang, a physician in Plano, Texas, who is from China. She discussed some of the desperate needs of the children she'd seen while overseas. He followed up on her phone call, and after several Texas doctors agreed to volunteer their services, five children requiring radical cranial surgery were flown from China to the United States. Marcy, along with Dr. Chang and other well-wishers, waited at the airport to offer their support to the children who would undergo the life-changing operations.

Through her experiences as Nurse Ducky, Marcy has discovered that laughter has *eternal* as well as *internal* benefits. It is an amazing medicine created by God—a potent and powerful therapy for the soul as well as for the physical body. When we laugh, endorphins flow, our hearts beat a little easier, and God floods our spirits with peace.

Best of all, refills are unlimited. And they don't come with childproof caps!

The Bible says that in heaven, there is no sickness or pain. Could that be because heaven is filled laughter? As Martin Luther once said, "If you are not allowed to laugh in heaven, then I don't want to go there."

I have a feeling he is laughing right now.

In fact, when the thunder roars just before a steady, hard rain, I wonder if it isn't actually the thunderous rumble of laughing saints rocking heaven's pearly gates.

Keep your face with sunshine lit,

Laugh a little bit!

Gloomy shadows oft' will flit

If you have the wit and grit

Just to laugh a little bit!

—*Anonymous*

Wing Tip

$\mathcal{L}$aughter is universal, life-giving, and contagious! You never know where a joyful heart might lead you. Deliberately spread some joy and goodwill today and watch it multiply.

If we love

one another,

God lives in us

and his love

is made complete

in us.

—1 John 4:12

If instead of a gem, or even a flower,

we should cast the gift of loving

thought into the heart of a friend,

that would be giving as the angels give.

—George MacDonald

Chapter 9

SWEET potato BLESSINGS

Betty Pickitt and her husband (I just always called him "Pickitt") lived two houses down from my family when I was a child growing up in East Texas. I remember going to Betty and Pickitt's house every day on my own, just to say hello or to see what Betty might be cooking on her old wood stove.

Everything always smelled so good at Betty and Pickitt's. I especially remember the sweet potatoes. It seemed like every time I went for a visit, those sweet potatoes would be baking and almost ready to eat. "Sugar," Betty would say, "you're just in time for some mighty good vittles!"

The fact that Betty and Pickitt were black and I was white never registered in my little four-year-old mind. I loved them like most kids love a grandmother and grand-daddy. They were my friends, and I felt safe and always welcome at their house. Sometimes they would read me a story from the well-worn Bible that often lay open on their kitchen table. They took time to answer my questions, and I remember feeling that they always wanted me to stay just a little longer. Many times Betty would send me home with a few still-warm, baked sweet potatoes tucked under my small arms. She'd say, "Now you run on home and take these to your mama." I really felt like I had done something good when I handed Mama those sweet potatoes!

One day when I arrived at home, Mama got a dish-towel and wiped fresh sweet potato off my mouth. "Why is it that you won't ever eat sweet potatoes when *I* cook them?" she asked.

"They just taste better at Betty's house," I explained simply. Maybe it was the old wood stove she cooked them in, or perhaps it was the way she heaped on fresh butter and a pinch of salt. Whatever the reason, I can remember their unique taste that, to this day, has never been matched. Even more, I can picture Betty's smiling face as she handed me a plate and then winked at Pickitt, watching me intently as I devoured the much-appreciated feast. I never remember a visit when Betty didn't have something cooked and ready to serve. Giving was a way of life for them.

Some days Pickitt would stop by our house on his way into town. When Mama answered the door, Pickitt would tip his hat and ask, "Ma'am, is there anything I can bring you from town?"

"No, but thanks for asking," Mama would usually say.

"Well, then, Ma'am," Pickitt would continue, "do you mind if I bring back a little somethin' for Miss Suzie?"

"That'll be fine," Mama always replied.

Pickitt would then lean down, smile that big smile of his, and say, "And what would Miss Suzie like ol' Pickitt to bring her from town today? Will it be candy corn or cashew nuts?"

I remember sitting on the front porch steps, eagerly awaiting Pickitt's return, and thinking, *I must be special to Betty and Pickitt*. I realize now that we indeed shared a special friendship—one that defied age and race, a friendship born of the spirit from which love, acceptance, peace, and joy flow. Such friendship does not recognize prejudice or status in life; it recognizes only that which the voice of the heart calls "real." When Pickitt handed me my much-anticipated package and I said, "Thank you, sir," it seemed to make his day!

I remember being fascinated by the turkeys Pickitt raised behind their house. The big birds made such funny noises! One day when Pickitt was out feeding them, I said, "It sounds like those turkeys are talking."

"Why, sure they are, Miss Suzie," he said. "They're talkin' turkey talk."

"Can you understand what they're saying?" I asked.

"Sometimes I can," Pickitt answered.

My curious childhood imagination took over as I continued to probe. "What are they sayin' right now?"

Pickitt knelt down until he was even with me, looked straight into my wide eyes of wonder, and said, "Why, Miss Suzie, I do believe those turkeys are sayin' how glad they are to see you. That's why they make so much commotion when you come around."

Believing every word that he spoke, I waved to the whole flock and exclaimed, "I'm very glad to see you too!"

Pickitt chuckled out loud, patted me on the head,

and said in his usual way, "Oh, Miss Suzie, you just won't do."

A few days later on yet another visit, Pickitt called me over to the turkey pen and pointed to the young turkeys that were roaming about. "You know, Miss Suzie, Thanksgiving will be coming up in a few months, and I've just been thinkin' that you might like to pick out a turkey of your own for me to raise just for you," he said. I quickly pointed to the one I thought was the very best. Pickitt pulled a colored string out of his overall pocket and handed it to me.

"Well, all right now," he said, "let's catch him and tie this string to his leg so we'll know for sure which one is Miss Suzie's turkey."

I never gave the fate of the doomed bird a thought. I was too caught up in the excitement of Pickitt letting me capture and tag my own Thanksgiving turkey. I felt proud, as if a special honor had been bestowed upon me. He suggested we name the bird Tom. In the weeks that followed, my daily visits found me looking anxiously inside the pen for Tom, the grandest turkey in the yard, with the red string tied to his leg. Pickitt told Mama about our adventure and that she could be expecting ol' Turkey Tom around Thanksgiving.

103

Although the friendship between a Southern white child and an old black couple was an unlikely one in the early fifties, that relationship became a bridge, closing one gap in an all-too-prejudiced society. With wisdom, humility, and a servant's heart, Pickitt was able to give gifts through me to my family and we were able to give back to them. I couldn't have known at the time all that I was being taught in the process. But somehow I think Betty and Pickitt did. I also believe they were old enough and wise enough to learn some simple lessons from me too.

Tucked away inside my grown-up heart is a childhood smile that escapes and makes its way to my lips every time I remember my special friends. Strange as it may seem, one of the first things I want to do when I get to heaven is look up Betty and Pickitt. I have a feeling their mansion will be easy to find. I'll just look for the smoke curling from the chimney and follow my nose to their door—where I know, inside, sweet potatoes will be cooking in an old wood stove. And I expect a kind and gentle face will greet me and say, "Why Miss Suzie, we've been waiting for you, sugar. Come on in and let me fix you a plate."

There are no friends like old friends,
And none so good and true;
We greet them when we meet them,
As roses greet the dew;
No other friends are dearer,
Though born of kindred mold;
And while we prize the new ones,
We treasure more the old.

—*David Banks Sickles*

Wing Tip

Do you recall a friend from your childhood who influenced your life in a special way? Someone who gave you simple and delightful gifts of encouragement, acceptance, and love that you'll always cherish? Remember, the treasures you pour into the heart of a friend today will last forever.

It is more blessed

to give

than to receive.

—Acts 20:35

It is wonderful to think

what the presence of one human being

can do for another—

change everything in the world.

—*George S. Merriam*

Chapter 10

WHAT can I DO?

At times it grew quiet in the neonatal intensive care unit of Dallas's Parkland Hospital. Quiet except for the gentle motion of a rocking chair and the soft music playing from a tabletop radio. Quiet except for the rhythmic breathing of a tiny infant wrapped in the soft folds of a sky blue blanket. Quiet except for the soothing words Terence Elliott whispered to the fragile soul he cradled in his arms: "You're a beautiful boy. Who knows, you just might be the next Beethoven or Einstein."

It was a familiar scene inside the neonatal unit, where doctors and nurses scrambled to save the lives of critically ill newborns. Terence wasn't a doctor, but a calm serenity could be felt whenever he arrived in the ward.

He was there to do something the doctors and nurses seldom had time to do.

He was there to rock the babies.

For seven years Terence Elliott volunteered an average of twenty hours a week in the neonatal unit and became an invaluable asset to doctors, nurses, and patients alike. He changed diapers, helped the nurses with their duties, and spent hour after hour rocking, walking, and holding premature and seriously ill babies—some of whom had no chance of survival. He often wept with grieving parents when they were given bad news about their children.

A visiting newspaper reporter once described the babies in the intensive care unit as "wrinkly bits of flesh and hair wrapped in blankets." Many were no longer than an adult's outstretched hand, their weight measured not in pounds and ounces but in grams.

"What do you feel when you hold one of these tiny creatures?" the reporter asked Terence. "It's very unusual to see a man volunteering in the neonatal unit and holding babies. Why do you do it?"

"I feel blessed to be a part of their lives," Terence answered. "Some will improve and go home to live with their parents, but some will not. Many babies here are born to drug-addicted mothers, and others are born to parents who don't want them. Even loving parents are sometimes afraid to bond with their critically ill babies. But they are all tiny angels, and even the ones who will not survive deserve to know love—if only for a few hours or days before they are given back to the heavenly Father."

In a sense Terence became their surrogate parent, wrapping his babies in love and warmth and giving them something they wouldn't otherwise have. Many were the times a tiny soul with only hours to live nestled close to the only parent he or she would know on this earth. Terence made sure the precious infants in his care didn't feel alone. He'd move next to the radio so the babies could hear gentle music along with his soothing voice. He'd let them feel the touch of a butter-soft kiss upon their tender cheeks. For however many moments or hours the babies lived, Terence gave them the blessing of love.

Where does such love come from?

"I have no answer except that it's something God put within me," he says.

Even Terence is surprised at the compassion that

moves him to give to others. "At times it's so strong, it feels like Niagara Falls—it's that powerful," he explains. "But it's exciting to think God can do that."

Terence and his wife, Patti, were never able to have children of their own. But Terence believes God gave him many children to care for. Children have always been drawn to Terence, and he to them. "Jesus had a kinship with children," Terence notes. "They are all so very special."

A native of Australia, Terence vividly remembers the prayer he voiced when he was ten years old. "Our Father," he prayed, "what can I do?" At that moment he was gripped with a compelling conviction that he could make a difference in the world. God needed his help! He was certain that he was on this earth for a purpose: to serve mankind.

The inexplicable compassion he felt, even for strangers, was overwhelming at times. Terence could hardly wait until he turned seventeen, the legal age in Australia for donating blood. So on his seventeenth birthday, he began his lifelong service as a blood donor and hospital volunteer. Terence was twenty-four when he moved to America to begin his career as a geophysicist and geology consultant. But his passion for being a blood donor and a volunteer nurse's aide never wavered.

"No feeling in the world compares to curling up and laying your head on a pillow at night, knowing you might have saved someone's life," Terence says.

He's been called a hero. But Terence is uncomfortable with any hint of praise about his mission of serving others. Employees at Parkland Hospital had to secretly nominate him for the Volunteer of the Year Award, knowing he would refuse the nomination if he knew about it. He won the award three years in a row but adamantly refused a fourth nomination, wanting others to be recognized for their service. Once he was named Employee of the Month—even though he'd never been on the hospital payroll.

"I've never met anyone like him," says Laura Elms, who headed up the Parkland neonatal unit when Terence was there. "He was the volunteer, and we should have been thanking him. But he always looked out for us and our well-being."

Another coworker, Lisa Little, adds: "'Earth angel' is the perfect description for Terence Elliott. He's donated more blood to help children than anyone I know of."

One year Terence donated blood forty-eight times at three different institutions. Over several years' time, he gave a total of forty gallons to the Dallas blood supply for children.

Terence is still known as Parkland Hospital's single biggest blood donor. When he found out the hospital's most desperate need was for blood platelets for children with cancer and leukemia, he stopped giving away his whole blood and began giving blood platelets instead— a much more tedious and time-consuming process.

There were many times when Terence's blood was the only thing keeping a child alive. "I never wanted anyone to know I was their donor," he says. "I just wanted to help."

He remembers one terminally ill ten-year-old who needed three units of white blood cells over a ten-day period. "I knew that in her particular case, the blood wouldn't ultimately save her," he recounts, "but it would provide more precious time for her and her mother. And that was reward enough."

In 1995 Terence received Dallas's prestigious Savvy Award and the Dallas County Individual Volunteer of the Year Award—both on the same day. But Terence says that he has received something far greater than human recognition: "The Father's assurance that I had been doing His will." At the public ceremony Terence graciously accepted the awards, hoping, he said, that "sleeping souls might be inspired to become a volunteer or blood donor and awaken to the vast opportunities that are waiting out there for their help."

Terence is no longer volunteering at Parkland Hospital. A few years ago he and Patti relocated to Natchitoches, Louisiana, where they opened a bed-and-breakfast. The charming, historical town, much smaller and slower-paced than Dallas, offered the perfect ambiance for a quieter lifestyle. But rather than slowing down, Terence found that there is no rest from your soul's truest passion.

Soon after getting settled, Terence went to an old pre-Civil War cemetery to pray. He was surprised to hear, rising from a place deep within his soul, the prevailing prayer he'd prayed as a ten-year-old child: "Our Father, what can I do?" It wasn't long before Terence was volunteering again—in the local emergency room, often pulling twelve-hour shifts; in the newborn nursery; and with the hospice-care program.

The thirsty cry of Terence Elliott's heart to do something for God and for others cannot be quenched—and he constantly looks for new ways to serve. "I never feel as if I've done enough. I want to do so much more," he says. "If people could only understand what potential they have, what they have to give to others, it would free them and free the people they're giving to. And the world could be a very different place."

Terence relates his passion to the passion of Oskar Schindler in the award-winning movie *Schindler's List.* After being told he'd done so much during the Holocaust years to save so many Jews, Oskar spoke from a mournful heart, "I didn't do enough." In that scene, Oskar thinks of all the moments he squandered and opportunities he wasted when he could have helped more people.

Today when Terence visits the old cemetery—his praying place—he thinks of lives lost and lives yet to be saved. Now sixty years old, he prays not only for the needs of the people he encounters daily but also for himself—that he will live long enough to touch even more lives.

"I'm only one person, but there is so much that one person can do," he says with conviction. "If each of us realizes what infinite power we have within to help mankind, we will understand that we all belong to each other—and we are here to make a difference."

Perhaps some of us will never have the opportunity to do such heroic acts as a Terence Elliott or an Oskar Schindler. However, the Hebrew inscription inside the ring Oskar was given—a quote from the Talmud—imparts a great message to us all: "He who saves one life, saves the world entire."

Lord, make me an instrument of your peace:

Where there is hatred, let me sow love;

Where there is injury, pardon;

Where there is doubt, faith;

Where there is despair, hope;

Where there is darkness, light;

Where there is sadness, joy.

Lord, may I not so much seek to

Be consoled as to console;

To be understood as to understand;

To be loved as to love.

Because it is in giving that we receive,

In pardoning that we are pardoned.

—*Saint Francis of Assisi*

Wing Tip

$\mathcal{N}$ever miss an opportunity to give. Even one stone, when cast upon the water of service to others, creates far-reaching ripples. Whatever you do to lessen another's burden makes a difference in that person's life—and in the world!

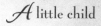A little child

will lead them.

—Isaiah 11:6

In the old days there were angels

who came and took men by the hand,

and led them away from the city of destruction.

We see no white-winged angels now.

But yet men are led away from threatening

destruction: a hand is put into theirs,

which leads them forth gently toward

a calm, bright land,

so that they look no more backward;

and the hand may be a little child's.

—George Eliot

Chapter 11

OUT OF THE mouths OF babes

During my first year of writing, I rarely shared anything I'd written with friends or family members. While I worked at sharpening my writing skills, I privately wondered if I'd ever be brave enough to reveal to others the words I'd penned.

But one day while visiting my daughter's family, my little granddaughter, Kara, asked what kind of story I'd been writing lately.

"Well, I have one with me," I said. "It might be boring to you, but I'll read it if you like."

"Yes! Please read it to me," she replied enthusiastically. Kara sat down on her pink quilted bedspread as I fumbled through a satchel to find a manuscript I'd recently finished. My daughter, Kelly, joined us, and the three of us sat cross-legged on Kara's bed while I read a simple short story about picking wildflowers. The narrative was rather reflective and, I thought, not one a typical eight-year-old could relate to. I was sure Kara would grow restless before I reached the end. To my great surprise, however, she listened intently until the story was over.

Nervously, I waited for what was sure to be Kara's all-too-candid yet innocent critique.

"Well—what do you think?" I finally asked.

Kara pursed her tiny rosebud lips; turned her big, blue, twinkling eyes toward her mother; and said matter-of-factly, "Well, well, it looks like we have ourselves a little writer on our hands!"

Kelly and I burst out laughing. When we regained our composure, I hugged Kara close and kissed her little cherub face. My laughing tears quickly gave way to tender tears of pure bliss.

It was a moment that will be forever framed upon the wall of my heart. Kara's precious words of affirmation nestled warmly in the soft folds of my writer's soul. They became hallowed seeds of endorsement that were both planted and watered by an eight-year-old angel.

From Kara's viewpoint, my writing was real and valuable. And in that moment I became more than an aspiring writer. I became *her little writer*—"little" in the sense that Kara's words of endearment and innocent patronage would serve to somehow keep me humble. I was now officially confirmed to the world of writing and bound to fulfill her trust. I was *Kara's little writer*, and I would guard those credentials with my very heart.

Many are the stories of great men and women who were inspired by the words of other great men and women—words credited for making them the people they became. But in one brief moment I discovered that the age of the lips from which those words are spoken (or the hand by which they are written) doesn't matter. Words have real power to emit life. They possess the power to heal or destroy, bind or set free, discourage or encourage, love or hate. Simple words of affirmation are a lighthouse in a sea of doubt.

Even when they're from a child. Author Margaret Lee Runbeck wrote, "Of all the dear sights in the world, nothing is so beautiful as a child when it is giving something. Any small thing it gives. A child gives the world to you. It opens the world to you as if it were a book you'd never been able to read…. A child has so little that it can give, because it never knows it has given you everything."

No endorsement in the world could ever compare to the one given to me by a little angel who unknowingly took my heart in her hands and erased any lingering doubts I had about writing. Kara's innocent words and childlike faith ended my floundering search for significance in the writing world. It took only one sentence from an eight-year-old with no agenda, formula, or selfish motive to fan the flames of my deepest longings and aspirations.

Now on days when I'm feeling overwhelmed by the pressures of life and, yes, the stress that often accompanies a writing deadline, I close my eyes and recapture the gift of Kara's precious words. Once again, a pen sprinkled with angel dust inscribes across the pages of my heart: *I'm somebody's little writer.*

In the world of harried adulthood, it's all too easy to lose our sense of wonder and excitement and forget what is necessary to live simply, passionately, and deliberately. But kids have it right. I'm convinced that if we follow their lead, a trail of crumbs and small bits of wisdom spoken from a pure heart will lead us ever closer to the kingdom of God.

Pen from Heaven

Pen from heaven, write to me,
Words of what the Master sees.
Take my hand and let it flow
As a servant of my soul.

Pen from heaven, speak to me,
Oracles of sweet simplicity.
Take my laughter; take my pain,
And write for me of heaven's gain.

Pen from heaven, please impart
The words I need to write my heart.
From where celestial angels throng,
Pen from heaven, write the song.

Write the story, write the prose;
Write to me from where love grows.
Master author, closest friend,
Write to me from heaven's pen.

—Susan Duke

*C*hildren are natural encouragers. Accept their offerings of spontaneous insight as the pure and priceless gifts that they are—and look to their childlike faith as an example of the kind of faith that touches the heart of God.

Sing to the LORD

a new song;

sing to the LORD,

all the earth.

—Psalm 96:1

Lord, let me give and sing and sow and do my best,

Though I in years to come may never know what

soul was helped thereby.

Content to feel that thou canst bless all things however small

To someone's lasting happiness, so, Lord, accept my all.

—Prudence Tasker Olsen

Chapter 12

angel IN A BLUE vest

It was 1944. Angry waves crashed against the sides of the ship bound for South Hampton, England, where Ray Winter and thousands of American soldiers were scheduled to land. As the ship rocked violently, Ray became so ill he wondered if he would even make it to shore. With every ounce of strength he could muster, he whispered a prayer: "Lord, if I make it back home alive, I promise I'll sing for You."

The moment the ship landed, Ray was taken to sick bay. Not only had Ray been unmercifully seasick, the ship's doctor also determined that he had the mumps. So while Ray's comrades in the Ninety-sixth Chemical

129

Motor Battalion journeyed onward to their assigned mission in Germany, Ray was left behind in the military hospital.

Within days, the shocking word came that the entire Ninety-sixth Battalion had been wiped out.

Why? Ray asked himself. *Why was my life spared?*

Ray realized his heart-wrenching question might never be answered. But he remembered the promise he'd made aboard his ship—a promise he was destined to keep.

As a child Ray had loved singing with his father in church. But now as an adult, he had no idea where his promise to sing might lead him. He only knew that God had spared his life, and he was convinced that singing was his true mission and calling.

Although most singers require scheduled engagements and a platform or podium from which to sing, Ray needed none of these to fulfill his promise. He simply determined to sing from the depths of his heart wherever and whenever the opportunity arose. While working as a maintenance man and groundskeeper for the Creek County Courthouse in Oklahoma, Ray could often be heard singing joyously throughout the building. His coworkers were amazed—both at his boldness to belt out a tune and the richness of his velvety baritone-bass voice.

Through the years, other singing opportunities presented themselves to an always-willing Ray Winter. He sang in nursing homes, for benefits, or wherever he was needed. When he finally retired from his job at the courthouse, he was certain he still had more singing to do. And in 1994—fifty years after promising God that he would sing—Ray found another unlikely singing platform.

Ray was hired as a greeter at the Wal-Mart Supercenter in Tulsa, Oklahoma, where he dons his blue vest four days a week. But Ray's greetings go far beyond a gentle smile or nod of the head as customers enter the store. In fact, many customers greet him first if they catch him in one of his rare, quiet moments.

"Hey, Ray! Do you have a song for me today?" asks a young woman with four kids in tow.

"Why, sure I do!"

A pudgy, middle-aged man with a glowing smile walks past Ray, grabs a shopping cart, and calls out, "Ray, could you sing 'Amazing Grace' while I'm here?"

Ray never hesitates to oblige his customers, many of whom have become like family to him. Hymns are his favorites, but occasionally he sings one of his spirited, original, and spontaneous Wal-Mart jingles, accentuating his deep bass voice when he sings about "low, low" prices!

He never knows how his singing might impact a customer's heart. One afternoon a pretty lady named Monica walked up to Ray as she was leaving the store. "I was feeling so tired and down when I came in here today," she told him. "But when I heard you singing, my spirit began to soar, my step became lighter, and my whole mood changed. Thank you, Ray! Thank you for your songs and the ministry from your heart!"

Ray's value to the store was underscored when his wife suggested that he ask for a transfer to a Wal-Mart that was closer to their home. Ray went to his manager with the request, which certainly seemed reasonable. But to Ray's surprise, the manager asked, "What will it take to keep you *here?*"

Ray had always worked the night shift and Sundays without complaint. But seizing the moment, he asked, "How about the day shift and Sundays off?"

"You got it!" the manager replied without hesitation.

Obviously, Ray has never been shy about publicly displaying his God-given talent. He believes a gift shouldn't be hidden under a bushel. "If you're doing what God called you to do and you're making people smile, being timid makes no sense," he says.

Once Ray and his wife went to Branson, Missouri, where the famous singing group The Platters was performing live onstage. When the group asked for a volunteer from the audience to come up and sing with them, guess who stood up.

"Ray, you're the first one ever to take us up on our request!" they said. "Do you know Tennessee Ernie Ford's 'Sixteen Tons'?"

"Sure do!" And with that, Ray became, for a few moments at least, the sixth Platter. Ray was such a hit, the Platters gave him a standing invitation to sing with them whenever he was in town. The next time he visited Branson, he went prepared, bringing along a bright red jacket that was perfect for blending in with The Platters' show-biz attire.

Now seventy-eight years young, Ray Winter knows from experience that God provides countless mission fields on which to use the gifts He has given us. He also knows that true ministry does not take place only behind stained-glass windows.

Sometimes God uses ordinary men to tend to matters of the heart. And if one thing has been proven through the ages, it's this: Hearts need to be sung to.

"There are many ways someone can make a difference in this life. Mine just happens to be singing in Wal-Mart," Ray says. "I'm the one who's blessed when a customer comes up to me and says something like 'You made me smile' or 'You just made my day.' Well, *that* makes *my* day! Some have even come back into the store and told me that they've committed their life to the Lord. And that's the greatest joy of all."

No doubt the angels in heaven agree. And no doubt they dance and clap and sing along whenever they hear a silver-haired angel in a blue vest lifting his voice from the busy doorway of the Wal-Mart Supercenter in Tulsa, Oklahoma.

(Look for Ray Winter's first CD titled *The Singing Wal-Mart Man*—available you-know-where!)

A Song of Service

If all my pain and all my tears,
And all that I have learned
Throughout the years
Could make one perfect song
To lift some fallen head
To light some darkened mind,
I should feel that not in vain
I served mankind.

—Marguerite Few

Wing Tip

Always keep a song tucked away in your heart. You never know when someone may need a heavenly dose of music for her soul.

$\mathcal{B}$e careful not to

do your "acts of

righteousness" before men,

to be seen by them.

—Matthew 6:1

The noblest service

comes from unseen hands,

And the best servant

does his work unseen.

—Oliver Wendell Holmes

Chapter 13

THE ANONYMOUS angel

You won't catch him riding on a tall, white stallion named Silver or mysteriously covering his eyes with a black mask. But his *hair* is silver and *he* is tall—about six feet, by most estimates. And his late-model pickup truck—a more modern means of transportation than that of the famous masked television hero, the Lone Ranger—is white.

There are other similarities. Like his legendary, fictitious counterpart, this soft-spoken, well-dressed, sixty-something mystery man is a hero to many, spreading good will and generosity in the hearts of unsuspecting townspeople of all ages. No one knows his true identity

—at least no one willing to tell—and you never know just where or when he might show up in the dusty West Texas town of San Angelo.

When Bernice first encountered the kindhearted gentleman, she was volunteering at the Sante Fe Crossing Senior Citizen Center. After her husband died, she discovered that she loved working and interacting with the people at the center and started helping out on a regular basis. She'd just finished serving lunch one day when a man walked up to her and handed her a white envelope.

"When you get home, there's something inside just for you," the stranger said before he turned and walked away.

Bewildered, Bernice simply stared at the envelope. Finally her friend Juanita, who was standing nearby, insisted, "Bernice, open it! Aren't you curious to see what's inside?"

Bernice nervously opened the envelope and gasped when she found a crisp fifty-dollar bill and a pink card with the scripture from Matthew 5:8 written inside. She read the passage out loud: "Blessed are the pure in heart, for they will see God."

The gift brought tears to Bernice's eyes. But the

bearer of the gift disappeared before she could thank him. Bernice gave half of the money to her church and half to the senior citizen center. "The gift gave me such joy, I wanted to pass it on to someone else," she explains.

Knowing she couldn't rest until she found a way to thank the kind stranger, Bernice decided to contact Rick Smith, a reporter and staff writer for the *San Angelo Standard Times*. She told him what happened and went on to explain her dilemma. "Somehow," she said, "I want this man to know that it touched my heart to find out there are people like him in the world."

Rick honored Bernice's request by writing the first article about the mystery man. To his surprise, others who had encountered the benevolent stranger began to come forward with stories of their own. A lady named Susan informed Rick that the mystery man had visited her and handed her a white envelope while she was holding a garage sale in her yard. Long after the gentleman was gone, she pulled the envelope from her apron pocket and found a crisp fifty-dollar bill and Matthew 5:8 written on a pink card.

Did the stranger have any clue that during the previous two years, Susan's life had been riddled with illness and the death of loved ones? For her, the envelope had more than monetary and momentary value. She was greatly comforted to know that someone cared and that angels must surely be watching over her.

"I'll keep the envelope, money, and card on my desk forever," she says, "as a reminder during spiritual emergencies that there are still good people in the world."

While San Angelo citizens have been trying to figure out the identity of the mysterious man and why he hands out fifty-dollar bills and scriptures to strangers, the anonymous angel continues his mission of charity and good will. From a young nineteen-year-old mother of a newborn baby to a co-coordinator for Meals for the Elderly, recipients have been graced by the anonymous angel at times in their lives when they seemed to need encouragement the most. No one knows if this particular factor is a coincidence; but then, is anything a coincidence—really? When people think quickly enough to ask who he is before he slips away, Mr. Angel simply says it isn't necessary for them to know.

What has actually been happening in San Angelo, Texas? A man with a mission has been inadvertently teaching some valuable and timeless lessons of the heart. Susan says she's used what happened and how it happened as an example to her daughter of how people can do good things in quiet ways. She's pointed to the mystery man to show that we don't always have to be told "thank you" for the things we do. It's nice to hear those words, but people who do good deeds receive their own reward deep within their hearts.

Another lady who called the newspaper office said her envelope experience made her think about giving more to others. "I can't go around handing out fifty-dollar bills, but I can find one person to give fifty dollars to who really needs it," she said. In fact, she was planning to give the money to a particular woman at Christmas. "That fifty dollars won't make or break me," she said, "but it will mean the world to her."

It seems everyone who has received a white envelope has been blessed, whether they needed the money or not. Like Susan, one man decided to keep the fifty dollars, explaining, "I just can't believe someone would actually do something like this for me." The envelope represented a sacred moment—a moment that would forever make him feel chosen and blessed.

After writing numerous articles about the anonymous angel in the newspaper, Rick Smith attempted to close the book on the mysterious phenomenon. But each time he thought the story had run its course, he'd hear from another thankful beneficiary. Rick couldn't help but wonder about the identity of the man who was inspiring so much of his journalism—although many people told him that "unmasking" the stranger might ruin things or spoil the angel's mission. Rick published an open letter asking the now locally renowned mystery man for yet one more blessing: an explanation. But there was no response.

I became enamored with this story when I first heard about and researched it. I didn't care if I ever found out the anonymous angel's name, but I did want to talk with him and find out the motivation behind his secret giving. I wanted to hear his heart. And to do that, I knew I must hear his voice.

So what does a stumbling, bumbling angel like myself do when she wants to find an anonymous angel who lives miles away across the state of Texas? She prays.

And guess what? As sure as the golden sun sets in the West Texas sky, someone (who shall remain nameless) sent me what they thought might be the angel's phone number. My fingers shook as I picked up the phone, praying that the numbers I pressed on the dial pad would lead me to the man I'd heard so much about—

and that he'd be willing to talk to me. After his "Hello," for the next few minutes, all I heard was the sound of my own nervous voice explaining that I was writing a book and assuring the silent angel on the other end of the line that I would respect his anonymity and never ask his name.

"I just want to hear your heart," I said softly. "I think you have an amazing story. But I want to know more."

To my surprise, San Angelo's angel confirmed that I'd found him. He talked with me for more than forty-five minutes. What did I find out? That he was indeed kindhearted. That he had good reasons for wanting to remain anonymous. That he was inspired by God to begin his mission. That he'd suffered the loss of a dear wife. And that he gets great joy when he knows his act of kindness has touched someone in a special way.

He also said that the scripture on each pink card— Matthew 5:8—was divinely inspired. Why did God lead him to use that particular verse? He wasn't sure.

"Perhaps the pure in heart are those who receive your gift with a pure motive," I suggested. "And perhaps that verse is God's way of showing them the pure intention of your heart too."

"Perhaps," said the anonymous angel.

"How do you choose who receives the envelopes?" I probed cautiously.

"I don't choose them," he said. "When I go out each day, I have no idea where to go. But I'm very aware that I'm being led to certain individuals. It may be someone picking up cans on the side of the road or someone sitting on a park bench. It may be someone who is dirty and bedraggled or someone who looks well off. I've felt led to pull into garage sales, retirement centers, and churches. Sometimes it's as if the person is 'highlighted' to me, and I'm always surprised."

"How long do you plan on doing this?" I asked.

"At least a year, and then I'll see if I feel that God wants me to continue."

During the rest of our conversation, the anonymous angel shared more of his heart. He spoke openly about God, life, love, and loss. He told me why he started his mission and why he fulfills his mission with such ardent dedication. Then he gave me permission to reveal all that he shared.

But something happened after I hung up the phone. I knew unquestionably that I had spoken to an earth angel. I'd been allowed to enter the inner sanctum of his heart without reservation. Strangely, I felt as if I'd just tread upon sacred, holy ground.

So I made a decision.

Out of respect and reverence for a gentleman I may never meet face to face, I determined that some mysteries are too hallowed to be unveiled.

I need not shout my faith. Thrice eloquent
Are quiet trees and green listening sod;
Hushed are the stars, whose power is never spent;
The hills are mute: yet how they speak of God!

—*Charles Hanson Towne*

Wing Tip

$\mathcal{T}$rue generosity is giving with
no expectation of thanks in return.
Think of someone to bless and
encourage secretly—and enjoy the
reward of your own heart being
filled with delight!

Weeping may remain

for a night,

but rejoicing

comes in

the morning.

—Psalm 30:5

We are each of us angels

with only one wing.

And we can only fly

embracing each other.

—Luciano De Creschenzo

Chapter 14

WHEN angels CRY

"Do you think angels cry?" a chubby-cheeked, dark-haired little boy asked me one day while I stood in a grocery-store checkout line. I'd felt him peering at me as I fumbled through my purse for my checkbook and flipped through magazines from the counter's display rack. When I finally looked down at him, his large, chocolate eyes drew me helplessly into their realm of wonder and eager appeal. He appeared to be about four years old—and anxious for my reply.

"Well, yes," I stammered. "I'm sure angels must cry sometimes."

"When? Like, when somebody dies?" my curious little friend quizzed.

"Yes. I think when we're sad about someone who dies, angels must surely cry with us."

"I think so too," the child spoke confidently. "I think the angels cried when my grandma died."

"Is that because you cried for your grandma?" I asked, hoping to show this inquisitive and talkative little boy that I was interested in what he had to say.

"Yep. I cried a lot. And I think the angels cried lots too. I think they stopped everything they were doing and just cried for a long, long time. They help us cry so we don't have to feel sad for so long."

"I'm sure you're right. You must have loved your grandma very much."

"Yep. She was my best friend. Have any angels ever cried with you?"

I swallowed hard, trying to push back the lump that had suddenly found its way to my throat. How could I respond without an inappropriate display of emotion in front of this innocent, unsuspecting child? Perhaps a simple answer would be the best way to end our conversation as we inched nearer the checkout.

"I think so," I said softly yet guardedly.

"Who did you love that died?"

"My son," I answered, silently praying I wouldn't have to say anything more.

"I'll bet he misses you a lot. Do you miss him? How old was he?"

"Yes, I miss him—very much," I said in a whisper, choking back tears. "He was eighteen."

"I could tell you knew about the angels," the little boy offered enthusiastically.

"Oh? And how could you tell?" I asked with honest curiosity as I wiped a straying tear.

"Because you smile kind of like my grandma did, and she's the one who first told me about them."

I knew, in his own way, my little grocery-store friend had just given me a special compliment. And during our brief but divine encounter, he'd found a fellow believer to support his faith.

I reached to lightly brush his hand. "Thank you," I said. "I'm glad your grandma told you about the angels."

By the time our conversation ended, a middle-aged gentleman, whom I presumed to be the young boy's grandfather, paid for his groceries and reached for his grandson's hand. As they walked out through the automatic glass doors, the little boy turned and gave me a quick wave and a smile.

For the rest of the day, I thought about the uncanny wisdom wrapped in this young boy's inquisitive words. And I wondered what his grandma told him about the angels. Was she preparing him for grief? Did she know she was dying and that he'd be left without his best friend? What exactly *did* she tell him about angels crying?

Whatever she told him, he had taken it to heart. And unbeknownst to him, he'd become an unlikely angel of comfort in that grocery-store checkout line. The things he shared made me remember all of the earth angels who stopped what they were doing and cried along with me when I was grieving so deeply: the youth group that came to decorate our Christmas tree that first Christmas without Thomas; the friend who left a single red rose at my door that first Mother's Day; the friend who sent me a card every week for more than a year.

Angels who cried with me and shared my sorrow. Angels who embraced me and lent me their wings, their tears, and their prayers.

"Do you think angels cry?"

I'll never forget those words.

Yes, I believe heavenly angels cry when we cry. And I believe God surrounds us with earthly angels who help us cry too—so we don't have to feel sad for so long.

Angel Tears

When we weep, do the heavens weep too?
Perhaps they do, I've heard it's true.
And when we're sad, do angels descend
And find their disguise in the eyes of a friend?
Do angels dance, and do they weep?
Do they wipe our tears and sing us to sleep?
I'm certain angels with heavenly wings
Sometimes do these earthly things,
But earth angels are those held so dear
Who lend us their wings and share our tears.

—*Susan Duke*

Wing Tip

*T*ake time to listen to the innocent wisdom and encouragement of
children. Your listening will fuel
their faith, and their perceptions will
bring healing to your soul.

The LORD

has done

great things

for us,

and we are filled

with joy.

—Psalm 126:3

When you finally allow yourself

to trust joy and embrace it,

you will find you dance with everything.

—Emmanuel

Chapter 15

JOY TO THE world

As soon as we spied the first guests turning into the driveway, Judy and I ran out onto her charming Victorian front porch, positioned ourselves audaciously on the top two steps, and began joyfully belting out the "Hallelujah Chorus."

"Hallelujah, hallelujah…Hallelujah! Hallelujah! Hal—leee—lu—jah!"

We were a bit off-key, but we didn't care. The grins and giggles from the ladies getting out of their cars only heightened our spirited enthusiasm. What a sight we were: two forty-something women dressed up in home-made angel attire, complete with puffy wings of white tulle and sparkly, golden halos. Our guests stared, staggered, and sashayed their way up the red-brick path leading to Judy's front porch, their faces registering everything from utter shock and dismay to bubbling jubilation.

"We're your heavenly hostesses today!" we declared as we ushered each lady inside to our second annual After-Thanksgiving Tea, a special party for all the women in our family and their invited guests. The house smelled of spiced tea, freshly baked sugarplum cake, and cranberry candles. Judy's dining table was set with her best dishes, finger sandwiches, and all the trimmings for an elegant and delectable lunch.

I suppose the women weren't all that surprised to see Judy and me dressed as angels. They knew we are both little girls at heart. In fact, people have always commented on how much Judy and I are alike. Her mother and mine were expecting us at the same time. I was born in June; Judy, in July. The fact that her father was my half brother made me her aunt when I was a mere one-month-old! We had fun growing up together and have remained close through the years. Sometimes our eyes still twinkle just like they did when we were giddy four-year-olds stirring up delicious mud pies enriched with sugar, cinnamon, and Kool-Aid!

The After-Thanksgiving Tea was Judy's idea. Thanksgiving is our designated family-reunion time, with the traditional meal usually served at Judy's parents' house. Each year Judy and I wait until the family has feasted on turkey and the men are all comfortably positioned in their armchairs for an afternoon of football. Then we sneak away to her house a few miles down the road. That's when we catch up on each other's lives over a cup of hot tea and simply while away the afternoon in her old porch swing.

But for several years, sitting on Judy's front porch, we found ourselves asking each other the same question: "Why can't Thanksgiving be different? It's great being with family; but all we do is eat, go our separate ways, and it's over. Where's the meaning? The tradition? The spiritual and emotional bonding?"

It troubled us.

Then, as another Thanksgiving approached, Judy called me. "Suzie, I've had a brainstorm," she said. "I know what we can do about Thanksgiving this year! You'll have to help me pull it together, but I think we can do this."

"What are you talking about?" I asked.

"You know how we've longed for Thanksgiving to be different—to have more meaning and tradition? Well,

I've been thinking. If it's ever going to be different, we're going to have to be the ones to change things. We've been waiting for someone else to do something, but we're the ones who love making memories and encouraging people. So maybe *we're* the ones who should start a new tradition.

"What do you think about having a tea party at my house the day after Thanksgiving for all the women in the family?" she continued excitedly. "They can even invite guests. I'll prepare a variety of finger sandwiches, vegetable dips, and desserts. We'll exchange small gifts, and I'll give a devotional. You can sing and read us one of your stories. Won't this be a wonderful way to start the Christmas season?"

"It sounds great," I said, "but it also sounds like a lot of work for you. Besides, do you think anyone will actually come? We'll be competing with the after-Thanksgiving sales!"

"Suzie, it really doesn't matter how many women show up. We need this—and everyone else does too. They just don't know it yet! I think an after-Thanksgiving tea party will encourage our families to be closer and give us something to look forward to. So how about it?"

Of course, I couldn't refuse. Judy was right. We had griped and complained for years. Now, instead of remaining a part of the problem, we could be part of the solution.

My daughter, Kelly, Judy's daughter, Amanda, and Judy's sisters, Cindy and Loretta, agreed to help with the party. That first year we were thrilled when close to thirty enthusiastic family members and friends showed up. The laughter and tears we shared were a dream come true for Judy and me. A fresh tradition had been birthed.

The next year I was the one with the brainstorm. Judy and I had already decided that the theme for the second annual tea would be angels. Everyone would bring an angel gift or ornament to exchange. But then another idea came to me.

Just a few days before Thanksgiving, I called Judy long-distance. "I know something that will perfectly complete the theme for our tea this year," I said excitedly. "Since you and I are hosting, we can dress up as 'heavenly hostesses'— you know, in angel outfits!"

"Oh Suzie, you've got to be kidding," Judy objected. "I'm so busy getting everything ready at my house, I don't have time to find angel outfits!"

"Don't worry. I'll gather up all the stuff," I promised.

"I don't know how yet, but by Thanksgiving, I'll have our heavenly attire ready."

"Girl, I don't know about this," Judy laughed. "But I'm game if you are!"

I'm constantly amazed at the way God takes one little idea and turns it into a small bit of heavenly manna to be shared with others. For instance, I never expected what happened at the local Wal-Mart Supercenter when I went shopping for our angelic apparel. After I found some white sheets, I selected a roll of white bridal tulle from the fabric department and asked the lady at the cutting table to measure and cut six yards.

"Someone getting married?" the fabric clerk asked.

"No ma'am," I replied.

"Well, I've noticed that people are using this stuff to wrap baskets and make bows. It does make great bows, doesn't it?"

"I wouldn't know. I've never made bows with it," I said.

"Well, I'm sure there are all sorts of things you can use this stuff for—potpourri sachets, dish scrubbers, and who knows what."

The inquisitive lady obviously wanted to know why I was buying six yards of white tulle. I just wasn't sure I was brave enough to tell her.

Finally she asked me outright: "Well, what *do* you plan on doing with this stuff?"

"Actually, I'm going to try to make some angel wings," I admitted.

"Oh? Is one of your children in a play?"

"No, as a matter of fact, *I'm* going to be the angel."

The fabric clerk's dark red eyebrows sprang up like two tightly rolled window shades, and her eyes shouted, *Lady, are you for real?*

Feeling I owed her some sort of explanation at that point, I told her about the family tea party and the angel theme. A few moments later her eyes began to glisten, and soft tears trickled down her ruddy cheeks.

"I'm sorry. I don't know why I'm crying," she said. "This just sounds like such a wonderful idea! I have three sisters in town, and we never get together anymore. We used to be close, but after our mom died a few years ago, we sort of drifted apart. I've been wondering lately how I could reach out and show them how important it is for us to be close again. You've inspired me to call them and invite them over for a tea party."

She wiped her eyes. "You just don't know how this has made my day! If fact, it's beginning to feel like Thanksgiving to me for the first time in years!"

A few days later I arrived at Judy's house, angel costumes in tow. We had such fun getting ready—we made a precious memory even before the tea began! We giggled like kids playing dress-up, fluffing our wings, shaping our halos, and lacing up our tennis shoes (which we made sure *weren't* covered by our robes). Judy wore red high tops, and I wore my white Reeboks—part of the uniform for fast-running angels, we reasoned. Judy's angel name became Holly because her last name is Wood and she wanted to be Miss Hollywood. Mine was Leon, which is *noel* spelled backward—since backward is the direction I'm apt to be flying most of the time. We thought we'd been close before; after that morning, we were celestially bonded!

Our mothers, daughters, sisters, aunts, nieces, and cousins came to the tea, and everyone had a wonderful afternoon. Each woman got her picture made with the angels. The photograph of my mom and me is framed and sits where I can see it even now as I type. Another one of Judy and me chasing each other around a tree reminds me that the kid in both of us is still alive and well. May we never get too old or too staid in our ways to be a little bit silly!

As it turned out, our angel costumes got quite a workout that day. When all the guests had gone home, Judy's sister Cindy asked us to go to the hospital in our angel garb to visit a cousin who hadn't been able to take off from work that day. We agreed—but only if she'd dress up and go with us. So the three of us, in all our homemade glory, along with a few other relatives, piled into a jeep and drove to the hospital. The strange looks we got at red lights and again when we entered the hospital made us wonder if someone might call security on us!

We packed into an elevator and pushed the sixth-floor button. On the way up, however, the doors opened on the second floor. A lady waiting there for the elevator took one look at us—and screamed.

"Fear not!" I said as the doors closed again in front of her.

By the time we got to the lab where our cousin Jackie worked, we were so giddy we were afraid we might get thrown out of the hospital. But Jackie, who laughed and thanked us for coming to see her, had plans for us. She knew of a couple of special patients who needed cheering up—and she was sure three angels were just the thing to do it.

In fact, one of the patients was a sixteen-year-old girl named Sarah who loved collecting angels. She was just coming out of a coma after a serious automobile accident. As we appeared at her bedside and sang "Hark! The Herald Angels Sing," we could see her sweet eyes silently telling us "thank you." Several months later Sarah called Judy to let her know that she was finally home and doing fine—and that she'd always remember the real-life angels who came to sing to her in the hospital. Her mother also got on the phone and told Judy that she could never express how much joy our visit had brought at such a critical time in their family's life.

In another room we sang to a man who had only weeks to live. He laughed at the mere sight of us! He loved to laugh, his wife told us. So we asked him to sing along with us on a special rendition of "Hark! The *Hairy* Angels Sing." He was still laughing out loud when we left the room. His wife followed us outside, grabbed our hands, and with tear-filled eyes thanked us over and over for the visit.

Funny what a couple of sheets and a few yards of tulle can do! When I shared the pictures from the tea party with a friend back in my hometown, she asked me to put on the angel outfit once again and go with her to visit a friend who was in dire need of cheering up. She brought her own homemade cardboard wings, and we trotted off on our angel-mission of mercy. That's a whole other story that would take too long to tell. But I will tell you this—thinking about it makes me want to sing the "Hallelujah Chorus" all over again!

Everyone needs an angel sometimes. And I've learned something new since I first took that flying leap into angel territory. *Real* angels have their work cut out for them! They certainly don't need the help of daring, fun-loving impersonators, but it's awesome to see what God can do with a little imagination! To be a pretend angel, even for a little while, was a joy unlike any I think I've ever experienced. It's one of those ideas that happen to turn out right—and one that keeps on making my heart smile.

C. S. Lewis once wrote, "Joy is the serious business of heaven." My angel wings and I agree. That's why I keep them hanging in my closet, just in case I'm called to active angel duty again. For I've learned a valuable truth over the years: Joy shared brings a double blessing. Opportunities to spread a little cheer in this world are heaven's mandate—and earth's reward.

I Believe in Angels

I believe in angels!
I think they're everywhere!
And when life's sorrows are really tough,
I think God sends a pair.
One for each side to prop us up
Where we're too weak to stand,
To steady us and guide us,
And to lend a helping hand.
Two more hearts for courage,
Four more eyes to help us see
That God is right above us
Listening to every plea!
Four more feet to carry us
When we think we can't go on;
Two more souls to encourage us
So we know we're never alone.
So when the winds of life blow through
And bring storm clouds to your day,
Don't be discouraged because
God has an angel on the way.

—Margie Lynn Whitehead

Wing Tip

Joy is like a bubbling, effervescent spring that can't help but flow out to others. Spreading it is one of the greatest blessings you have been given here on earth—and vitally refreshing to your own soul.

An Irish Blessing

May God grant you many years to live
for sure he must be knowing
the earth has angels all too few
and heaven's overflowing.

SOURCES

Every effort has been made to trace the sources for all poems used in this book. We regret any errors or oversights and will be pleased to make necessary corrections in future editions.

Introduction: Earning My Wings
Excerpt from "Influence" by Joseph Norris. *The Treasure Chest*, New York: Harper Collins, 1995, 131.

Chapter 1: The Last Straw
Untitled poem by unknown author. *The Sword Scrapbook*, Viola Walden, comp., Murfreesboro, Tenn.: Sword of the Lord Publishers, 1969, 41.

Chapter 2: Soaking Wet at the Circle K
Excerpt from "A Gentle Heart" by J. R. Miller. *Streams in the Desert II*, Mrs. Charles E. Cowman, ed., Grand Rapids, Mich.: Zondervan, 1996, 349.

Chapter 3: A Key of Compassion
Excerpt of poem by John Vance Cheney. *Leaves of Gold*, Fort Worth, Tex.: Brownlow, 1948, 81.

Sources

Chapter 5: Highway to Heaven
Excerpt of hymn, "All the Way My Savior Leads Me," by Fanny J. Crosby. Public domain, 1875.

Chapter 6: Touched by an Angel's Prayer
"The Unseen Bridge" by Gilbert Thomas. *The Treasure Chest*, New York: Harper Collins, 1995, 169.

Chapter 7: Major Memo
Excerpt from an anonymous poem. *Streams in the Desert*, Mrs. Charles E. Cowman, ed., Grand Rapids, Mich.: Zondervan, 1965, 338.

Chapter 8: Nurse Ducky and the HaHa Team
Excerpt from an anonymous poem. *Today is Mine*, Fort Worth, Tex.: Leroy Brownlow, 1972, n.p.

Chapter 9: Sweet Potato Blessings
Excerpt of poem by David Banks Sickles. *A Forever Friend*, Eugene, Oreg.: Harvest House, 1998, 46.

Chapter 10: What Can I Do?
"The Serenity Prayer" by Saint Francis of Assisi (1182–1226).

Chapter 12: Angel in a Blue Vest
"A Song of Service" by Marguerite Few. *The Treasure Chest*, New York: Harper Collins, 1995, 102.

Chapter 13: The Anonymous Angel
Untitled poem by Charles Hanson Towne. *The Joyful Heart Flip Calendar*, Edina, Minn.: Heartland Samplers, Inc., 1994.

Chapter 15: Joy to the World
"I Believe in Angels" by Margie Lynn Whitehead. Copyright 1994. Used by permission.

SHARE STORIES OF THE
earth angels
IN YOUR LIFE

If the stories in *Earth Angels* have encouraged you in any way or if you have a story you'd like to share, Susan would love to hear from you.

Susan is also available for speaking engagements and may be contacted at:

Susan Duke
P.O. Box 8025
Greenville, Texas 75404

E-mail: suzieduke@juno.com

For more information see Susan's Web site at www.suzieduke.com

Other great Heartlifters® books

Heartlifters for Teachers
ISBN: *1-58229-158-6*

Heartlifters for Friends
ISBN: *1-58229-100-4*

Heartlifters for the Hurting
ISBN: *1-58229-202-7*

Heartlifters for Hope and Joy
ISBN: *1-58229-074-1*

Heartlifters for Sisters
ISBN: *1-58229-203-5*

Heartlifters for Women
ISBN: *1-58229-073-3*

Other great Hugs™ books